THE LITTLE
BEAN
COOKBOOK

THE LITTLE
BEAN
COOKBOOK

SMITHMARK

This edition published in 1996
by Smithmark Publishers,
a division of U.S. Media Holdings, Inc.,
16 East 32nd Street
New York, NY 10016

Smithmark books are available for bulk purchase
for sales promotion and premium use. For details write
or call the Manager of Special Sales,
Smithmark Publishers
16 East 32nd Street
New York
NY 10016
(212) 532-6600

ISBN 0-7651-9816-9

Publisher: Joanna Lorenz
Senior Cookery Editor: Linda Fraser
Assistant Editor: Emma Brown
Copy Editor: Jenni Fleetwood
Designer: Lilian Lindblom
Illustrator: Anna Koska
Photographers: Karl Adamson, Michael Michaels, James Duncan, Steve
Baxter, Amanda Heywood, Patrick McLeavey, David Armstrong,
Michelle Garrett & Edward Allwright
Recipes: Christine France, Roz Denny, Annie Nichols, Carla Capalbo,
Frances Cleary, Soheila Kimberley, Laura Washburn, Shehzad Husain,
Ruby Le Bois, Rosamund Grant, Liz Trigg, Alex Barker, Carole Clements,
Elizabeth Wolf-Cohen, Rafi Fernandez

Printed in China
10 9 8 7 6 5 4 3 2 1

Contents

Introduction

Packed with protein, gentle on the wallet, convenient and easy to prepare, pulses are the perfect choice for today's cook. Dried beans and lentils are astonishingly versatile, playing a starring role in appetizers, soups, salads and casseroles. Every nation has its own favorite recipes, from France's cassoulet to Mexico's chili con carne. In China and Japan dried beans are even used to make desserts.

The popularity of pulses dates from early in man's history. Esau's porridge was a bowl of lentils, and beans were used by the ancient Romans to cast votes, white beans signifying aye and colored beans nay. During the feast of Saturnalia, a bean was used to decide who should preside over the festivities, a custom which survived in Britain in the baking of the

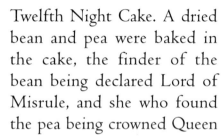

Twelfth Night Cake. A dried bean and pea were baked in the cake, the finder of the bean being declared Lord of Misrule, and she who found the pea being crowned Queen for the duration of the festivities.

In countries where a large proportion of the population does not eat meat, such as India, pulses have always been a very important part of the national diet. The West has had a more ambivalent attitude; pulses were valued during World War II, but their popularity lessened once meat was again readily available.

The situation has reversed once more during the last decade or so. Today, pulses are very definitely back on the menu, prized for being high in fiber and lower in fat that any other protein food. To make the most of pulse protein, it should be combined with a starch (such as rice, pasta or bread), with nuts or seeds (especially sesame seeds or cashews), or dairy protein. These combinations occur naturally in recipes like Pasta and Bean Soup, Bean and Nut Salad, and Red Beans and Rice.

In many of the recipes that follow, other types of bean may be substituted for those suggested. Don't be afraid to experiment; every bean has its own character and you may well find you prefer the earthy taste of red kidney beans or the subtle sweetness of aduki. When substituting one type of bean for another, check cooking times, however, as these vary considerably.

Buy dried beans and lentils from a market or shop with a rapid turnover, and store them in airtight containers. Use within 9 months, before they start to shrivel and

harden. All pulses, except red split lentils and mung beans, must be soaked overnight in water before cooking. Follow the cooking times suggested, checking frequently to avoid overcooking or cooking the beans dry and burning them. Beans that are to be cooked again, in a soup or casserole perhaps, should be drained when they are just tender; beans intended for a purée should be soft but not mushy. The same goes for beans in salads — because they will firm up when cool, they need to be tender.

Many types of dried bean are readily available in cans — they are ready-cooked, which is a great time-saver for the busy cook. Take the time to get to know these, and the vast array of dried beans, and you'll discover a world of new recipe ideas.

Dried Beans & Pulses

ADUKI BEANS

Used for sprouting as well a stand-alone vegetable, these are small reddish-brown beans with a sweet, nutty flavor. Cook soaked aduki beans for 1–1½ hours.

BLACK BEANS

These shiny black beans, related to kidney beans, are very popular in Caribbean and Chinese cuisines. Cook soaked black beans for about 1 hour.

BLACK-EYED PEAS

Easily identified by the single black spot, these small beige legumes have a savory, earthy flavor. Cook soaked black-eyed peas for 30–45 minutes.

PINK BEANS

Attractive pinky-brown beans, these cook to a creamy consistency and are used for dips and salads, as well as bakes. Cook the soaked beans for about 1 hour.

LIMA BEANS

These flat pale-green beans have to be cooked carefully, as they quickly become mushy. They are very popular in salads, casseroles and curries. Cook soaked lima beans for about 1–1¼ hours.

CANNELLINI BEANS

Small and white, these are related to kidney beans. Use them in place of white beans or lima beans. Cook soaked cannellini beans for about 1 hour, or until tender.

CHICK-PEAS

Ranging in color from beige to golden brown, these beans (also called garbanzos) have a distinctive, slightly nutty flavor. They are delicious in dips (hummous), salads and curries. Cook soaked chick-peas for 1½–2 hours.

MUNG BEANS

Although best known for sprouting, green mung beans also make good eating. They cook quickly without soaking and are often puréed. Cook unsoaked mung beans for 30–35 minutes.

WHITE BEANS

This family of oval-shaped beans comes in a range of sizes, from the navy to the large Great Northern. The popular canned baked beans are white beans. Soaked white beans should be cooked for 1½–2 hours.

LENTILS

It is important to distinguish between green and brown lentils, which retain their shape after cooking, and red lentils, which cook down to a golden purée. Cook green or brown lentils for 30–45 minutes; red lentils cook in 20–25 minutes.

PINTO BEANS

Speckled or white, these medium-size beans have a floury texture when cooked and are a popular ingredient in soups and casseroles. Cook soaked pinto beans for 1½–2 hours, or until tender.

RED KIDNEY BEANS

These delicious, distinctive beans are an essential ingredient of chili con carne. Soaked dried red kidney beans must be boiled rapidly for 10 minutes at the start of cooking, then cooked for 1–1½ hours, or until tender.

SOYBEANS

High in protein, these beans can be boiled for consumption, but they are also used in soy milk and flour, tofu and soy sauce. The small hard beans need a long soak before being cooked for as long as 4 hours. Split soybeans are partially cooked, do not need soaking, and cook in about half an hour.

Techniques

PICKING OVER

Modern packaging means that most pulses have been carefully picked over, but it is still a good idea to spread them out and check for stones or twigs. Rinse in cold water and drain before soaking in a bowl.

SHORT SOAK

Tip the cleaned pulses into a saucepan, pour cold water over them to cover and bring to a boil. Boil rapidly for 3–5 minutes, then remove the pan from the heat and let sit for 1 hour.

SOAKING

The only pulses that do not need to be soaked in water before they are cooked are split red lentils and green mung beans, although even these will cook more rapidly if soaked. Place the pulses in a bowl and cover with cold water to twice their depth. Soak for 6–8 hours, or preferably overnight. Rinse the pulses well after soaking, as this helps to make them more digestible.

COOKING

Cook the drained pulses in 2–3 times their volume of water or unsalted stock. Bring the liquid to a boil, then lower the heat and simmer until tender (see pages 8–9 for timing). Add salt at the end of cooking; if added too soon salt will toughen the beans.

MICROWAVE COOKING

Pulses do not cook particularly well in the microwave, nor is there much to gain in terms of time. If you must cook beans and lentils this way, use a deep bowl, add plenty of boiling water and cook on High (100 per cent power) until tender. Check after two-thirds of the conventional cooking time. It is recommended that you do not cook red kidney beans by this method.

PRESSURE COOKING

You can save time by cooking soaked beans and lentils in a pressure cooker. Generally, the cooking time should be about a third of that stated for conventional cooking; consult the manufacturer's instructions for more information.

SPROUTING BEANS

Nutritious bean sprouts make a delicious addition to salads, sandwiches and stir-fries. To grow your own, you need a large, clean widemouthed jar, plus a circle of fine cheesecloth for a cover. Spoon dried aduki beans, mung beans or soy beans into the jar, filling it one-sixth full. Place the cover on top, securing it with a rubber band, then fill the jar with cold water. Drain well, then place the jar in a cool, dark place. Rinse and drain the beans daily. They will sprout in 2–3 days and will be ready to eat in less than a week.

11

COOK'S TIP

Buy beans for sprouting from health food shops to ensure that they are of good quality. Avoid using commercial seeds in case they have been treated with pesticides.

Soups & Appetizers

Pasta & Bean Soup

INGREDIENTS

1½ cups dried pink, pinto or
cannellini beans
14-ounce can plum tomatoes, chopped,
with their juice
3 garlic cloves, crushed
2 bay leaves
pinch of coarsely ground black pepper
6 tablespoons olive oil, plus extra
to serve (optional)
3 cups vegetable broth
2 teaspoons salt
1¾ cups ditalini or other small pasta
3 tablespoons chopped fresh parsley
freshly grated Parmesan cheese, to serve

SERVES 4–6

1 Soak the beans in water overnight. Rinse and drain well. Place the beans in a large saucepan and cover with water. Bring to a rapid boil and cook for 10 minutes. Rinse and drain again.

2 Return the beans to the pan. Add enough water to cover them by 1 inch. Stir in the chopped tomatoes with their juice, the garlic, bay leaves, black pepper and the oil. Simmer for 1½–2 hours, or until the beans are tender. Check the pan from time to time – if necessary, add more water.

3 Remove the bay leaves. Put about half the bean mixture into a blender or a food processor. Purée well. Pour into the pan with the remaining bean mixture. Add the broth and bring the soup to a boil. Stir in the salt and the pasta.

4 Cook until the pasta is *al dente*. Stir in the parsley. Allow to stand for at least 10 minutes before serving with grated Parmesan. (In Italy a little olive oil is poured into each serving.)

13

White Bean Soup

INGREDIENTS

*1½ cups dried cannellini or
other white beans
1 bay leaf
5 tablespoons olive oil
1 medium onion, finely chopped
1 carrot, finely chopped
1 stalk celery, finely chopped
3 medium tomatoes, peeled and
finely chopped
2 garlic cloves, finely minced
1 teaspoon fresh thyme leaves, or
½ teaspoon dried thyme
3 cups boiling water
salt and freshly ground black pepper
extra-virgin olive oil, to serve*

SERVES 6

1 Pick over the beans carefully, discarding any stones or other particles. Soak the beans in a large bowl of cold water overnight. Drain. Place the beans in a large saucepan of water, bring to a boil, and cook for 20 minutes. Drain. Return the beans to the pan, cover with cold water, and bring to a boil again. Add the bay leaf, and cook for about 1–2 hours, until the beans are tender. Drain again. Remove the bay leaf and discard it.

2 Purée about three-quarters of the beans in a food processor or blender, adding a little water if necessary. You may need to do this in batches.

3 Heat the oil in a large saucepan. Stir in the onion, and cook until it is tender. Add the carrot and celery; cook for 5 more minutes. Stir in the tomatoes, garlic  and thyme. Cook for 6–8 more minutes, stirring often until the mixture is thick.

4 Pour in all the boiling water. Stir in the beans and the bean purée. Add salt and pepper, then simmer for about 15 minutes. Serve in individual heated soup bowls.  Sprinkle each portion with a little extra-virgin olive oil, or offer this separately at the table.

14

Split Pea & Zucchini Soup

INGREDIENTS

1 cup yellow split peas
1 onion, finely chopped
1 teaspoon sunflower oil
2 zucchini, finely diced
3¾ cups chicken broth
½ teaspoon turmeric
salt and freshly ground black pepper
ciabatta or crusty bread, to serve

SERVES 4

16

1 Place the split peas in a bowl, cover with cold water and soak for several hours or overnight. Drain, rinse in cold water and drain again.

2 Cook the onion in the oil in a saucepan, stirring occasionally, until soft. Reserve a handful of diced zucchini and add the rest to the pan, stirring well.

3 Cook the zucchini mixture for 3 minutes, then add the broth and turmeric to the pan and bring to a boil. Reduce the heat, then cover and simmer for 30–40 minutes, or until all the split peas are tender. Stir in salt and pepper to taste.

4 When the soup is almost ready, bring a small saucepan of water to a boil, add the reserved diced zucchini and cook for 1 minute, then drain and add to the soup. Serve the soup hot with warm ciabatta or crusty bread.

COOK'S TIP

For a quicker alternative, use red lentils for this soup – they need no presoaking and cook very quickly. Adjust the amount of broth, if necessary.

Cauliflower, Flageolet & Fennel Seed Soup

INGREDIENTS

1 tablespoon olive oil
1 garlic clove, crushed
1 onion, chopped
2 teaspoons fennel seeds
1 cauliflower, cut in small florets
2 x 14-ounce cans flageolets,
drained and rinsed
5 cups vegetable stock
or water
salt and freshly ground black pepper
chopped fresh parsley, to garnish
toasted slices of Italian bread,
to serve

SERVES 4–6

2 Bring to a boil. Reduce the heat and simmer for 10 minutes, or until the cauliflower is tender.

I Heat the olive oil in a large saucepan. Add the garlic, onion and fennel seeds and cook for 5 minutes or until the onion softens. Add the cauliflower florets, half of the flageolet beans and the vegetable stock or water. Stir gently until well mixed.

3 Pureé the soup in a blender or food processor and return it to the pan. Stir in the remaining beans and season to taste. Reheat the soup and pour into heated bowls. Sprinkle with chopped parsley and serve the soup immediately, with toasted slices of Italian bread.

Bean Nachos

INGREDIENTS

2 tablespoons corn oil
2 onions, chopped
2 garlic cloves, chopped
3 jalapeño peppers, seeded and chopped
1½ tablespoons mild chili powder
16-ounce can red kidney beans, drained and
liquid reserved
3 tablespoons chopped fresh cilantro
1 large bag round tortilla chips
2 cups grated Cheddar cheese
½ cup pitted black olives,
thinly sliced
fresh cilantro sprigs, for garnishing (optional)

SERVES 8

1 Preheat the oven 425°F.

2 Heat the oil in a frying pan. Add the onions, garlic and jalapeños and cook for about 5 minutes, until soft. Add the chili powder and cook for 1 more minute.

3 Stir the beans into the onion mixture, then stir in ½ cup of reserved liquid from the beans. Cook for about 10 minutes, until thick, mashing the beans with a fork from time to time. Remove the pan from the heat and stir in the chopped fresh cilantro.

4 Put a little of the bean mixture on each tortilla chip. Top each nacho with a little cheese and a slice of olive. Arrange the nachos on a baking sheet.

5 Bake for 5–10 minutes, until the cheese has all melted and is beginning to brown. Serve at once, garnished with cilantro, if desired.

Falafel

INGREDIENTS

2 cups dried white beans
2 red onions, chopped
2 large garlic cloves, crushed
3 tablespoons finely chopped fresh parsley
1 teaspoon ground coriander
1 teaspoon ground cumin
1½ teaspoons baking powder
oil, for deep frying
salt and freshly ground black pepper
sliced tomatoes, to serve

SERVES 6

20

1 Soak the white beans overnight in water. Remove the skins and process in a blender or food processor. Add the chopped onions, garlic, parsley, coriander, cumin, baking powder and seasoning, and blend again to make a smooth paste. Cover the mixture and set it aside at room temperature for at least 30 minutes to firm up.

2 Flatten walnut-size pieces of the mixture to make small patties. Fry them in batches in very hot oil until golden, then drain. Serve hot, with sliced tomatoes.

COOK'S TIP

Falafel are usually made with chick-peas. For this version, use white beans or lima beans.

Hummous

INGREDIENTS

1 cup cooked chick-peas
½ cup tahini
3 garlic cloves
juice of 2 lemons
3-4 tablespoons water
salt and freshly ground black pepper
fresh radishes, to serve
GARNISH
1 tablespoon olive oil
1 tablespoon finely chopped fresh parsley
½ teaspoon paprika
4 black olives

SERVES 4–6

1 Place the chick-peas, tahini, garlic, lemon juice and seasoning in a food processor. Adding water as necessary, process the mixture to a very smooth paste.

2 Alternately, if you do not have a blender or food processor, pound the ingredients together in a small bowl until smooth.

3 Spoon the mixture into a shallow dish. Make a dent in the middle and pour the olive oil into it. Garnish with parsley, paprika and olives and serve with the fresh radishes.

COOK'S TIP
Canned chick-peas can be used for hummous. Drain and rinse under cold water before processing.

21

Salads & Vegetable Dishes

Bean & Nut Salad

INGREDIENTS

scant ½ cup red kidney, pinto or pink beans
scant ½ cup white cannellini or
lima beans
2 tablespoons olive oil
1 cup green beans, cut in
short lengths
3 scallions, sliced
1 small yellow or red bell pepper, sliced
1 carrot, coarsely grated
2 tablespoons crisp-fried onions or sun-dried
tomatoes, chopped
½ cup unsalted cashews or
halved almonds
salt and freshly ground black pepper
DRESSING
3 tablespoons sunflower oil
2 tablespoons red wine vinegar
1 tablespoon coarse-grain mustard
1 teaspoon sugar
1 teaspoon dried mixed herbs

SERVES 6

23

2 When cooked, drain and season the beans and toss them in the olive oil in a large serving bowl. Let cool for 30 minutes.

3 Add all of the other vegetables, including the sun-dried tomatoes, but not the fried onions, if using. Stir in half the cashews and toss to combine. Make the dressing by shaking the ingredients together in a jar. Toss with the salad and serve sprinkled with the fried onions, if using, and the remaining cashews.

1 Soak the beans overnight, if possible, then drain and rinse well, cover generously with cold water and cook according to the instructions on the package.

Warm Black-eyed Pea Salad

INGREDIENTS

1½ cups black-eyed peas
1 bay leaf
2 small red bell peppers
½ teaspoon Dijon mustard
2 tablespoons wine vinegar
¼ teaspoon salt
¾ teaspoon freshly ground black pepper
6 tablespoons olive oil
2 tablespoons chopped fresh chives
8 slices bacon, trimmed of fat
Italian parsley, to garnish

SERVES 4

1 Soak the peas, overnight if possible, then drain and rinse well. Cover the peas generously with cold water, add the bay leaf, and cook for about 30–45 minutes, until tender.

2 Preheat the broiler. Broil the peppers until charred on all sides, then steam them in a plastic bag for 10 minutes. Remove all the skin from the

peppers. Cut the peppers in half, discard the seeds, white membranes and stem, and slice them into ½-inch x 2-inch strips.

3 Combine the mustard and vinegar in a small bowl. Add the salt and pepper. Beat in the oil until well blended. Add the chives.

4 Cook the bacon until crisp. Drain on paper towels. Crumble the bacon into small pieces, set aside and keep warm.

5 When the peas are tender, drain them and discard the bay leaf. While they are still warm, toss them with the chive dressing. Mound the peas in a serving bowl. Sprinkle with the crumbled bacon and garnish with the strips of red pepper and a sprig of parsley. Serve warm.

24

Pinto Bean Salad

INGREDIENTS

1½ cups dried pinto beans, soaked overnight and
drained
1 bay leaf
3 tablespoons coarse salt
2 ripe tomatoes, diced
4 scallions, finely chopped
fresh cilantro or parsley, to garnish
DRESSING
¼ cup fresh lemon juice
1 teaspoon salt
6 tablespoons olive oil
1 garlic clove, crushed
3 tablespoons chopped fresh cilantro
freshly ground black pepper

SERVES 4

1 Put the beans in a large pan. Add cold water to cover and the bay leaf. Bring to a boil. Cover, and simmer for 30 minutes. Add the coarse salt and continue simmering for about 30 more minutes, until tender. Drain and let cool slightly. Discard the bay leaf.

2 Make the dressing. Mix the lemon juice and the salt with a fork, stirring until dissolved. Gradually stir in the oil until thick. Add the garlic, cilantro, and pepper to taste.

3 While the beans are still warm, place them in a large bowl. Add the dressing and toss to coat. Let the beans cool completely. Add the tomatoes, reserving some for the garnish, and scallions, and toss to combine. Set aside for at least 30 minutes before serving, garnished with the reserved tomato and fresh cilantro or parsley.

Tarka Dhal

INGREDIENTS

½ cup masoor dhal (split red lentils)
¼ cup moong dhal (small split
yellow lentils)
2½ cups water
1 teaspoon finely grated fresh ginger
1 teaspoon minced garlic
¼ teaspoon turmeric
2 fresh green chilies, chopped
1½ teaspoons salt
TARKA
2 tablespoons vegetable oil
1 onion, sliced
¼ teaspoon mixed mustard and
onion seeds
4 dried red chilies
1 tomato, sliced
GARNISH
1 tablespoon chopped fresh cilantro, plus
cilantro sprig
1-2 fresh green chilies, sliced
1 tablespoon chopped fresh mint

SERVES 4

26

2 Add the lentils to the water, with the ginger, garlic, turmeric and chopped green chilies. Cook for 15–20 minutes, or until soft. Stir occasionally.

3 Mash the lentil mixture to the consistency of a creamy soup. If the dhal mixture looks too dry, stir in more water. Season with the salt.

4 Make the tarka. Heat the oil and fry the onion with the mustard and onion seeds, dried red chilies and sliced tomato for 2 minutes.

5 Pour the tarka over the dhal and garnish with fresh cilantro, green chilies and mint.

COOK'S TIP

Dried red chilies are available in many different sizes. If the ones you have are large, or if you want a less spicy flavor, reduce the quantity to 1 or 2.

1 Pick over the lentils for any stones before washing them and draining them well. Pour the water into a saucepan and bring to a boil.

Tuscan Baked Beans

INGREDIENTS

3 cups dried beans, such as
cannellini
4 tablespoons olive oil
2 garlic cloves, minced
3 fresh sage leaves (if not available use 4 tablespoons chopped fresh parsley)
1 leek, finely sliced
14-ounce can plum tomatoes, chopped,
with their juice
salt and freshly ground black pepper

SERVES 6–8

1 Carefully pick over the beans, discarding any stones or other particles. Place the beans in a large bowl and cover with cold water. Soak for at least 6 hours, or overnight. Drain in a colander.

2 Preheat the oven to 350°F. Heat the oil in a small saucepan and sauté the garlic and fresh sage leaves or parsley for 3–4 minutes. Remove from the heat and set the pan aside.

3 In a heatproof casserole combine the drained beans with the leek and tomatoes. Stir in the oil with the garlic and sage. Add enough fresh water to cover the

beans by 1 inch. Mix well. Cover the casserole with a lid or foil, and place in the center of the hot oven. Bake for 1¾ hours.

4 Remove the casserole from the oven, stir the beans, and season with salt and pepper. Return them to the oven, uncovered, and cook for another 15 minutes, or until the beans are tender and dry-ing out a little on top to form a crust. Remove from the oven and allow to stand for at least 7–8 minutes before serving. This dish is excellent served either hot or at room temperature.

Stewed Lentils

INGREDIENTS

2 cups green or brown lentils
3 tablespoons olive oil
¼ cup pancetta or salt pork
1 onion, very finely chopped
1 stalk celery, very finely sliced
1 carrot, very finely chopped
1 clove garlic, peeled
1 bay leaf
3 tablespoons chopped fresh parsley
salt and freshly ground black pepper

SERVES 6

2 Add the celery and carrot and cook for 3–4 more minutes, stirring occasionally.

1 Carefully pick over the lentils, removing small stones or other particles. Place the lentils in a large bowl and cover with water. Soak for several hours. Drain. Heat the oil in a large, heavy saucepan. Add the pancetta or salt pork and cook gently for 3–4 minutes. Stir in the onion, and cook over low heat until it is soft, stirring the mixture frequently.

3 Add the lentils to the pan, stirring to coat them with the drippings. Pour in enough boiling water just to cover the lentils. Stir well, adding the whole garlic clove, the bay leaf and the parsley. Season with salt and pepper. Cook over medium heat for about 1 hour, until the lentils are tender. Discard the garlic and bay leaf. Serve hot or at room temperature.

Red Beans & Rice

INGREDIENTS

*3 cups dried red kidney beans,
soaked overnight
2 bay leaves
2 tablespoons oil or bacon grease
1 onion, chopped
2 garlic cloves, finely chopped
2 stalks celery, sliced
8 ounces salt pork or uncooked ham,
in one piece
2¼ cups long-grain rice
3 tablespoons chopped fresh parsley
salt and freshly ground black pepper*

SERVES 8–10

1 Drain the beans and put them into a large pan with fresh cold water to cover generously. Bring to a boil and boil rapidly for 10 minutes, then drain and rinse both the beans and the pan.

2 Return the beans to the pan with the bay leaves and fresh cold water to cover. Bring to a boil, then simmer for about 30 minutes. Add more water as needed.

3 Heat the oil in a frying pan. Cook the onion, garlic, and celery until soft. Stir the mixture into the beans and push the salt pork or ham into the middle.

4 Simmer, adding water as necessary, for another 45 minutes or so, until the beans are very tender. Add salt, if necessary, 15–20 minutes before the end of the cooking time.

5 Put the rice into a saucepan and add 1½ times its volume of cold water, plus 1 teaspoon salt. Bring to a boil, stirring occasionally. Cover the pan tightly and leave over very low heat for 12 minutes. Without lifting the lid, turn off the heat and leave the rice undisturbed for another 12 minutes (the rice should be cooked and all the liquid absorbed).

6 Remove the meat from the beans and dice it, removing the fat and rind. Drain the beans and add the diced pork. Season to taste.

7 Fluff the rice with a fork (if the rice has not absorbed all the liquid, drain the excess), stir in the parsley, then serve on a warmed platter, topped with the red beans.

Vegetarian Dishes

Potato-topped Bean Pie

INGREDIENTS

2¼ pounds potatoes
3 tablespoons extra virgin olive oil
1 large onion, chopped
1 green bell pepper, chopped
2 carrots, coarsely grated
2 garlic cloves, minced
3 tablespoons butter
1¼ cups mushrooms, chopped
2 x 14-ounce cans aduki beans, drained
2½ cups vegetable broth
2 bay leaves
1 teaspoon Italian seasoning mix
salt and freshly ground black pepper
dried bread crumbs or chopped nuts, to sprinkle

SERVES 6–8

2 Stir in the mushrooms and beans and cook for another 2 minutes, then add the broth, bay leaves and mixed herbs. Simmer for 15 minutes, stirring often. Preheat the broiler. Remove the bay leaves and transfer the vegetable mixture to a shallow ovenproof dish. Spoon the mashed potato over the top, spread it roughly, and sprinkle with the bread crumbs. Broil until golden brown.

1 Boil the potatoes until tender, then drain, peel and mash with the oil. Season. Fry the onion, pepper, carrots and garlic in the butter, until they are tender.

> ### COOK'S TIP
> Potatoes are easier to peel when boiled in their skins; this also preserves vitamins.

Turnip & Chick-pea Cobbler

INGREDIENTS

3 tablespoons sunflower oil
1 onion, sliced
2 carrots, chopped
3 medium turnips, chopped
1 small sweet potato or rutabaga, chopped
2 stalks celery, thinly sliced
½ teaspoon ground coriander
½ teaspoon Italian seasoning mix
15-ounce can crushed tomatoes
14-ounce can chick-peas
1 vegetable bouillon cube
salt and freshly ground black pepper
green leafy vegetables, to serve

TOPPING

2 cups self-rising flour
1 teaspoon baking powder
4 tablespoons margarine
3 tablespoons sunflower seeds
2 tablespoons grated Parmesan cheese
⅔ cup milk, plus extra for brushing

SERVES 4–6

1 Heat the oil and fry the vegetables for about 10 minutes until they are soft. Add the coriander, seasoning mix, tomatoes, chick-peas with their liquid and bouillon cube. Season well and simmer for 20 minutes. Pour the vegetables into a shallow casserole while you make the cobbler topping. Preheat the oven to 375°F.

2 Mix the flour with the baking powder, then cut in the margarine until the mixture resembles bread crumbs. Stir in the sunflower seeds and the cheese. Add the milk and mix until a firm dough forms. Gently roll out the topping to a thickness of ½ inch and cut out star shapes or circles or simply cut it into small squares.

3 Place the shapes on top of the vegetable mixture and brush with a little extra milk. Bake for about 12–15 minutes until well risen and golden brown. Serve hot with green, leafy vegetables.

34

Aduki Bean Burgers

INGREDIENTS

*1 cup brown rice (not the quick-
cooking variety)*
1 onion, chopped
2 garlic cloves, crushed
2 tablespoons sunflower oil
4 tablespoons butter
1 small green bell pepper, seeded and chopped
1 carrot, coarsely grated
*14-ounce can aduki beans, drained
(or ⅔ cup dried aduki beans, soaked
and cooked)*
1 egg, beaten
1 cup grated aged Cheddar cheese
1 teaspoon dried thyme
*½ cup toasted hazelnuts or toasted
slivered almonds*
whole-wheat flour or cornmeal, for coating
oil, for frying
salt and freshly ground black pepper
buns, tomato and lettuce, to serve

SERVES 12

1 Cook the rice according to the instructions on the package, overcooking it slightly so that it is soft. Drain the rice and transfer it to a large bowl. Fry the onion and garlic in the oil and butter, together with the green pepper and carrot, for about 10 minutes, until the vegetables are softened.

2 Add this vegetable mixture to the rice, together with the aduki beans, egg, cheese, thyme and nuts. Add plenty of seasoning. Chill until firm.

3 Shape into 12 patties, wetting your hands if the mixture sticks. Coat the patties in flour and set aside. Heat ½ inch of oil in a large, shallow frying pan and fry  the aduki burgers in batches until browned on each side, about 5 minutes total. Remove and drain on paper towels. Serve in buns with tomato and lettuce. Freeze any leftover burgers.

COOK'S TIP

*To freeze the burgers, cool them after cooking,
then open-freeze before wrapping and bagging.
Use within 6 weeks. Cook frozen burgers by
baking in a preheated 350° oven for
20–25 minutes.*

Red Bean Chili

INGREDIENTS

2 tablespoons vegetable oil
1 onion, chopped
14-ounce can crushed tomatoes
2 garlic cloves, minced
1¼ cups white wine
1¼ cups vegetable broth
2 thyme sprigs or 1 teaspoon dried thyme
2 teaspoons ground cumin
½ cup red lentils
3 tablespoons dark soy sauce
½ red chili, finely chopped
1 teaspoon pumpkin pie spice
8-ounce can red kidney beans, drained
2 teaspoons sugar
salt
steamed rice and corn, to serve

SERVES 4

2 Stir in the soy sauce, chili and pumpkin pie spice. Cover and simmer for 40 minutes, or until the lentils are cooked, stirring occasionally and adding more water if the lentils begin to dry out.

3 Stir in the kidney beans and continue cooking for 10 minutes, adding a little extra broth or water if necessary. Season with the sugar and salt to taste. Serve hot, with steamed rice and corn.

1 Heat the oil and fry the onion until soft. Stir in the tomatoes and the garlic. Cook for 10 minutes, then stir in the wine and the broth, thyme, cumin and lentils.

Kenyan Mung Bean Stew

INGREDIENTS

1¼ cups mung beans, soaked overnight
and drained
2 tablespoons butter
1 red onion, chopped
2 garlic cloves, minced
2 tablespoons tomato paste
½ green bell pepper, seeded and cubed
½ red bell pepper, seeded and cubed
1 green chili, seeded and finely chopped
1¼ cups water
salt and freshly ground black pepper

SERVES 4

2 Add the water, a little at a time, stirring well to blend all the ingredients together.

1 Cook the mung beans in water to cover, until soft and the water has evaporated. Mash coarsely and set aside. Heat the butter and fry the onion and garlic until golden, then stir in the tomato paste and cook for 2–3 more minutes, stirring. Add the mashed beans and the bell peppers and chili.

3 Return the mixture to a clean saucepan and simmer for about 10 minutes, then season and serve immediately in deep serving bowls.

COOK'S TIP

If you prefer a smoother texture, cook the mung beans until very soft, then mash them thoroughly until smooth.

39

Black-eyed Pea Stew with Spicy Pumpkin

INGREDIENTS

1¼ cups black-eyed peas, soaked for 4 hours
or overnight
1 onion, chopped
1 green or red bell pepper, seeded
and chopped
2 garlic cloves, chopped
1 vegetable bouillon cube
2 thyme sprigs or 1 teaspoon dried thyme
1 teaspoon paprika
½ teaspoon pumpkin pie spice
Tabasco sauce
2 carrots, sliced
1–2 tablespoons sunflower oil
salt and freshly ground black pepper
thyme sprigs, to garnish
SPICY PUMPKIN
2 tablespoons butter
or margarine
1½ pounds pumpkin, cut in cubes
3 tomatoes, peeled and chopped
1 onion, finely chopped
2 garlic cloves, crushed
½ teaspoon ground cinnamon
2 teaspoons curry powder
pinch of grated nutmeg
1¼ cups water
Tabasco sauce

SERVES 3–4

1 Drain the peas, place in a pan and cover generously with water. Bring the peas to a boil. Add the onion, green or red pepper, garlic, bouillon cube, thyme

and spices. Simmer for 45 minutes, or until the peas are just tender. Season to taste with salt and a little Tabasco sauce.

2 Add the carrots and oil and continue cooking for about 10–12 minutes, until the carrots are cooked, adding a little more water, if necessary. Remove from direct heat but keep hot until needed.

3 Make the spicy pumpkin. Melt the butter in a large frying pan or saucepan, and add all the pumpkin, tomatoes, onion, garlic, spices and water. Stir well to

combine and simmer until the pumpkin is soft. Season with Tabasco sauce, salt and black pepper, to taste. Serve with the black-eyed peas. Garnish the dish with thyme.

40

Bean & Barley Bowl

INGREDIENTS

3 tablespoons sunflower oil
1 red onion, sliced
½ fennel bulb, sliced
2 carrots, cut in sticks
1 parsnip, sliced
1 cup pearl barley
4 cups vegetable broth
1 teaspoon dried thyme
⅔ cup green beans, thinly sliced
15-ounce can pinto beans, drained
salt and freshly ground black pepper
chopped fresh parsley, to garnish
cheese croûtes, to serve (see Cook's Tip)

SERVES 6

1 Heat the oil in a heatproof casserole. Sauté the onion, the fennel, carrot sticks and parsnip slices for 10 minutes. Stir in the barley and broth. Bring to a boil, add the thyme and seasoning, then cover and simmer gently for 40 minutes.

2 Stir in the sliced green beans and drained pinto beans. Cover the casserole and continue cooking for another 20 minutes.

3 Ladle the bean stew into heated bowls, sprinkle with parsley, and serve, accompanied by cheese croûtes, if desired.

COOK'S TIP

To make cheese croûtes, slice a baguette, brush the slices with oil and place them on a baking sheet. Bake at 375°F for about 15 minutes, until light golden. Quickly rub each croûte with the cut halves of 2 garlic cloves. Top with 4 tablespoons grated Parmesan and return to the oven to melt the cheese.

Lima Bean & Pesto Pasta

INGREDIENTS

2 cups ditallini or other pasta shapes
grated nutmeg
2 tablespoons extra-virgin olive oil
14-ounce can lima beans, drained
3 tablespoons pesto sauce
⅔ cup light cream
salt and freshly ground black pepper
3 tablespoons pine nuts and
fresh basil leaves, to garnish
grated Parmesan cheese, to
serve (optional)

SERVES 4

43

1 Boil the pasta until cooked but firm (*al dente*), then drain, leaving it a little moist. Return the pasta to the pan, season, and stir in the nutmeg and oil.

2 Heat the beans in a saucepan with the pesto and the cream, stirring until it begins to simmer. Toss all the bean and pesto sauce into the pasta and mix well.

3 Serve in bowls, garnished with the pine nuts and basil. Serve with grated cheese, if desired.

Fish &
Shellfish Dishes

Tuscan Tuna & Beans

INGREDIENTS

2 tablespoons smooth Dijon mustard
1¼ cups olive oil
4 tablespoons white wine vinegar
2 tablespoons chopped fresh parsley, plus
extra to garnish
2 tablespoons chopped fresh chives, plus
whole chives to garnish
2 tablespoons chopped fresh tarragon or chervil,
plus extra sprigs to garnish
14-ounce can white beans
14-ounce can red kidney beans
1 red onion, finely chopped
8 ounce can tuna packed in oil, drained and
lightly flaked
sliced ciabatta or crusty bread, to serve

SERVES 4

1 In a small bowl, beat the mustard, oil, vinegar, parsley, chives and tarragon or chervil together.

2 Drain all the canned beans. Stir the chopped red onion, beans and tuna together in a bowl. Pour the dressing over the top and toss to combine. Transfer  to a large serving dish or individual bowls and garnish with the chives and fresh herbs. Serve at once, with slices of fresh ciabatta or crusty bread.

Roast Cod with Mixed Beans

INGREDIENTS

4 thick cod steaks
3 tablespoons sweet sherry or Madeira
14-ounce can pinto beans, drained
14-ounce can kidney or cranberry beans,
drained
2 garlic cloves, minced
1 tablespoon olive oil
1 teaspoon grated orange zest
2 tablespoons chopped fresh parsley
salt and freshly ground black pepper
strips of blanched orange peel and fresh
parsley sprigs, to garnish

SERVES 4–6

46

1 Skin the thick cod steaks and place them in a shallow dish. Pour on all the sherry or Madeira and marinate for 10 minutes. Turn the steaks once.

2 Preheat the oven to 400°F. Mix the beans with the garlic and place in the bottom of a heatproof dish. Place the fish on top and cover with the sherry. Brush the fish with the oil, then sprinkle with the orange zest, half the parsley and salt and pepper to taste.

3 Cover tightly with foil. Roast for 15–20 minutes. Pierce the thickest part of the fish with a knife to check if it is cooked through and continue cooking for another 2–3 minutes, if necessary.

4 Baste the fish with a little of the juices that collected in the foil during cooking. Serve the cod steaks and mixed beans immediately, on warmed plates. Sprinkle each serving with the rest of the chopped parsley just before serving, and garnish each portion with a few strips of orange peel and a sprig of fresh parsley.

Cod with Lentils & Leeks

INGREDIENTS

⅔ cup green lentils
1 bay leaf
1 garlic clove, minced
grated rind of 1 orange
grated rind of 1 lemon
pinch of ground cumin
1 tablespoon butter
1 pound leeks, thinly sliced or
julienned
1¼ cups heavy or whipping cream
1 tablespoon lemon juice, or to taste
1¼ pounds thick cod
or haddock fillet, skin removed
salt and freshly ground black pepper

SERVES 4

48

1 Rinse the lentils and put them in a large saucepan with the bay leaf and garlic. Add enough water to cover by 2 inches. Bring to a boil, and boil gently for 10 minutes, then reduce the heat and simmer for another 15–30 minutes, until the lentils are just tender and almost dry.

2 Drain the lentils and discard the bay leaf, then stir in half the orange zest and all the lemon zest, and season well with ground cumin and salt and pepper. Transfer to a shallow baking dish or gratin dish. Preheat the oven to 375°F.

3 Melt the butter in a saucepan over medium heat, then add the leeks and cook, stirring frequently, until softened. Add 1 cup of the cream and the remaining orange rind and cook gently for 15–20 minutes, or until the leeks are completely soft and the cream has begun to thicken. Stir in the lemon juice and season with salt and plenty of freshly ground pepper.

4 Cut the fish into four pieces. With your fingertips, locate and remove any small bones. Season the fish with salt and pepper, place it on top of the lentil mixture and press down slightly into the lentils. Cover each piece of fish with a quarter of the leek mixture and pour 1 tablespoon of the remaining cream over each piece. Bake for 30 minutes until the fish is cooked through and the topping is lightly golden. Serve the dish immediately; it needs no extra accompaniment.

Clam & Sausage Chili

INGREDIENTS

*1 cup dried black beans, soaked overnight
and drained*
1 bay leaf
1 teaspoon coarse salt
8 ounces lean sausage
1 tablespoon vegetable oil
1 onion, very finely chopped
1 garlic clove, crushed
1 teaspoon fennel seeds
1 teaspoon dried oregano
¼ teaspoon red pepper flakes, or to taste
2–3 teaspoons chili powder, or to taste
1 teaspoon ground cumin
2 x 16-ounce cans crushed tomatoes
½ cup dry white wine
*2 x 10-ounce cans clams, drained and
liquid reserved*
salt and freshly ground black pepper
Italian or soda bread, to serve (optional)

SERVES 4

1 Put the beans in a large pan. Add fresh cold water to cover and the bay leaf. Bring to a boil, then cover, and simmer for 30 minutes. Add the coarse salt and continue simmering for about 30 more minutes, until tender. Drain and discard the bay leaf.

2 Put the sausage in a heatproof casserole and cook over medium heat, for 2–3 minutes, until just beginning to brown. Stir frequently to break up lumps. Add the oil, onion, and garlic.

3 Continue cooking for about 5 more minutes, until the vegetables are soft, stirring occasionally.

4 Stir in the herbs, spices, tomatoes, wine and ¾ cup of the reserved clam juice. Bring to a boil, then lower the heat and cook, stirring occasionally, for about 15 minutes, or until the sauce is thick and full of flavor.

5 Add the black beans and clams and stir to combine. Continue cooking just until the clams are heated through. Adjust the seasoning, if necessary. Serve immediately, with slices of Italian bread or chunks of homemade soda bread, if desired.

Meat Dishes

Chicken with Herbs & Lentils

INGREDIENTS

1 slab (4 ounces) bacon,
rind removed, chopped
1 large onion, sliced
scant 2 cups chicken broth
1 bay leaf
2 each parsley, marjoram and thyme sprigs,
plus extra to garnish
1 cup green or brown lentils
4 chicken breasts or legs
salt and freshly ground black pepper
2-4 tablespoons garlic butter,
to serve (optional)

SERVES 4

53

1 Preheat the oven to 375°F. Fry the bacon gently in a heatproof casserole until it browns. Add the onion and fry until golden. Stir in the broth, herbs, lentils and seasoning.

2 Fry the chicken breasts in a nonstick frying pan until browned on both sides, then place them on top of the lentil mixture. Sprinkle with salt and pepper.

3 Cover the casserole and bake for about 40 minutes. Serve with a pat of garlic butter on each portion of chicken, if desired, garnished with a few herb sprigs.

COOK'S TIP

If your family doesn't like lentils use rice instead. For economy buy a small chicken and cut it into quarters, to give you four healthy portions.

Toulouse Cassoulet

INGREDIENTS

*2½ cups dried white beans (such as cannellini),
soaked overnight in cold water, then rinsed
and drained
1½ pounds Toulouse sausages
1 pound each boneless lamb and pork
shoulder, cut into 2-inch pieces
1 large onion, finely chopped
3 or 4 garlic cloves, minced
4 tomatoes, peeled, seeded and chopped
1¼ cups chicken broth
1 bouquet garni
4 tablespoons fresh bread crumbs
salt and freshly ground black pepper*

SERVES 6–8

1 Put the beans in a saucepan with water to cover. Boil vigorously for 10 minutes and drain, then return to a clean saucepan, cover with water and bring to a boil. Reduce the heat and simmer for 45 minutes, or until tender, then add a little salt and let stand in the cooking water.

2 Preheat the oven to 350°F. Prick the sausages, place them in a large heavy frying pan over medium heat and cook for 20–25 minutes until browned, turning occasionally. Drain on paper towels and pour off all but 1 tablespoon of the fat from the frying pan.

3 Increase the heat to medium-high. Season the lamb and pork and add enough of the meat to the pan to fit easily in one layer. Cook until browned, then transfer to a large dish. Continue browning the lamb and pork pieces, in batches.

4 Add the onion and garlic to the pan and cook for 3–4 minutes until just soft, stirring. Stir in the tomatoes and cook for 2–3 minutes, then transfer the vegetables to another dish. Add the stock to the frying pan, bring to a boil, then skim off the fat.

5 Spoon a quarter of the beans into a large casserole, and top them with about a third of the sausages, pork, lamb, and vegetables. Continue to layer in this way,  ending with a layer of beans. Add the bouquet garni and the broth and top with enough of the bean-cooking liquid to just cover.

6 Cover the casserole and bake for 2 hours (add more liquid if it seems dry). Uncover the casserole, top with the bread crumbs and press with the back of a spoon to moisten them. Continue to cook the cassoulet, uncovered, for about 20 more minutes, until browned. Serve at once.

Roast Leg of Lamb with Beans

INGREDIENTS

1 leg of lamb, 6-7 pounds
3 or 4 garlic cloves
olive oil
fresh rosemary leaves
2½ cups dried cannellini or flageolet beans,
soaked overnight in cold water
1 bay leaf
2 tablespoons red wine
⅔ cup lamb or beef broth
2 tablespoons butter
salt and freshly ground black pepper
watercress, to garnish

SERVES 8–10

1 First, preheat the oven to 425°F. Wipe the leg of lamb with damp paper towels and dry the fat covering well. Cut 2 or 3 of the garlic cloves into 10–12 slivers, then with the tip of a knife, cut 10–12 slits into the lamb and insert the garlic slivers into the slits. Rub with oil, season with salt and pepper and sprinkle with rosemary.

2 Set the lamb on a rack in a shallow roasting pan and cook for 15 minutes. Reduce the heat to 350°F and continue to roast for 1½–1¾ hours (about 18 minutes per pound). Baste the lamb occasionally.

3 Meanwhile, rinse the beans and put in a saucepan with enough fresh water to cover generously. Add the remaining garlic and the bay leaf, then bring to a boil. Reduce the heat and simmer for 45 minutes to 1 hour, or until the beans are tender, stirring occasionally and adding more water if needed.

4 Transfer the lamb to a board and let stand, loosely covered, for 10–15 minutes. Skim off the fat from the cooking juices, then add the wine and broth to the roasting pan. Boil over medium heat, stirring and scraping the bottom of the pan, until slightly reduced. Strain into a warmed gravy boat.

5 Drain the beans, discard the bay leaf, and toss the beans with the butter until it melts. Season with salt and pepper. Serve the lamb on a platter with the beans and garnish with watercress. Pass the gravy separately.

Hot & Sour Lamb & Lentil Curry

INGREDIENTS

4 tablespoons vegetable oil
5 green chilies, seeded and chopped
2 tablespoons grated fresh ginger
3 garlic cloves, minced
2 bay leaves
1 cinnamon stick (2 inches)
2 pounds lean lamb, cut into large pieces
2⅔ cups yellow split peas
2½ cups red lentils
2 potatoes, cubed and soaked in water
1 eggplant, cubed and soaked in water
3 sliced onions, deep-fried and drained
2 ounces frozen spinach, thawed and drained
1 ounce fresh or dried fenugreek leaves
2 carrots
2 cups chopped fresh mint leaves
4 cups chopped fresh cilantro
4 teaspoons garam masala
1½ teaspoons star anise powder
¾ teaspoon ground nutmeg
1½ teaspoons fenugreek powder
1 teaspoon mustard powder
2 teaspoons red chili powder
2 teaspoons brown sugar
4 tablespoons tamarind juice
salt and freshly ground black pepper
fried sliced garlic, to garnish

SERVES 4–6

1 Heat half the oil and sauté the chilies, ginger and garlic for 2 minutes. Add the bay leaves, cinnamon, lamb and 2½ cups water. Simmer until the lamb is half-cooked, then lift it out. Add the lentils to the pan and cook until tender. Mash roughly with the back of a spoon.

2 Drain the potatoes and eggplant and add to the lentil mixture with the deep-fried onion, the spinach, fenugreek and carrots. Add some hot water if the mixture is too thick. Cook until the vegetables are tender, then mash again, keeping the vegetables a little coarse.

3 Heat the remaining oil and gently fry the mint leaves and cilantro with the spices, sugar, salt and 1 teaspoon black pepper. Add the lamb and fry gently for 5 minutes. Return the spiced lamb to the lentil and vegetable mixture and stir well. Add liquid if necessary. Heat gently until the lamb is fully cooked.

4 Add the tamarind juice to the lamb mixture. Ladle into a serving dish and garnish with the fried garlic slices. Serve at once.

Lamb with Black-eyed Peas & Pumpkin

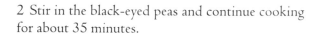

INGREDIENTS

1 pound lean boneless lamb, cubed
4 cups chicken or lamb broth or water
½ cup black-eyed peas, soaked for
6 hours or overnight, drained
1 onion, chopped
2 garlic cloves, crushed
2½ tablespoons tomato paste
1½ teaspoons dried thyme
1½ teaspoons vegetable oil
1 teaspoon pumpkin pie spice
½ teaspoon freshly ground black pepper
¾ cup pumpkin, chopped
Tabasco sauce
salt
boiled yam, plantain or sweet potatoes,
to serve (optional)

SERVES 4

2 Stir in the black-eyed peas and continue cooking for about 35 minutes.

3 Add the onion, garlic, tomato paste, thyme, oil, pumpkin pie spice, black pepper, salt and Tabasco sauce and cook for 15 more minutes or until all the beans are tender. Add the pumpkin and simmer for about 10 minutes, until the pumpkin is very soft and almost mushy. Serve with boiled yam, plantains or sweet potatoes, if you like.

1 Put the lamb in a large saucepan with the broth and bring to a boil, skimming off any foam, then reduce the heat, cover and simmer for 1 hour.

COOK'S TIP
Any dried white beans can be used instead of black-eyed peas. If you prefer a firmer texture, cook the pumpkin for just 5 minutes, until barely tender.

Black Bean Chili

INGREDIENTS

2 cups dried black beans, soaked overnight
and drained
2 tablespoons coarse salt
2 tablespoons vegetable oil
2 onions, chopped
1 green bell pepper, seeded and chopped
4 garlic cloves, minced
2 pounds ground beef
1½ tablespoons ground cumin
½ teaspoon cayenne, or to taste
2½ teaspoons paprika
2 tablespoons dried oregano
1 teaspoon salt
3 tablespoons tomato paste
2 x 14-ounce cans crushed tomatoes or
6 fresh tomatoes, chopped
½ cup red wine
1 bay leaf
chopped fresh cilantro, sour cream and grated
Cheddar cheese, to serve

SERVES 6

1 Put the beans in a large pan and add fresh cold water to cover. Bring to a boil, then cover and simmer for 30 minutes. Add the coarse salt and continue simmering for about 30 minutes or longer until the beans are tender. Drain and set aside.

2 Heat the oil in a large saucepan or heatproof casserole. Add the onions and pepper. Cook the vegetables over medium heat for about 5 minutes, until just softened, stirring occasionally. Stir in the garlic and continue cooking for about 1 more minute, stirring.

3 Add the beef. Cook over high heat, stirring frequently, until browned. Reduce the heat and stir in the cumin, cayenne, paprika, oregano and salt, mixing thoroughly.

4 Add the tomato paste, along with the tomatoes, black beans, wine and bay leaf and stir well. Simmer for 20 minutes and stir the mixture occasionally.

5 Check the seasoning. Remove the bay leaf and serve immediately, with the chopped fresh cilantro and sour cream. Pass the grated cheese separately.

Index

THE FINNS IN AMERICA

The IN AMERICA *Series*

THE **FINNS** IN AMERICA

ELOISE ENGLE

Published by
Lerner Publications Company
Minneapolis, Minnesota

For Jaakko Bergqvist,
a great friend of the Finnish-Americans

LIBRARY OF CONGRESS CATALOGING IN PUBLICATION DATA

Engle, Eloise Katherine.
The Finns in America.

(The In America Series)
Includes index.
SUMMARY: A survey of Finnish immigration to America
including their reasons for leaving their homeland, adjustment
problems here, and their contributions to almost every aspect
of American life.

1. Finnish Americans—History. [1. Finnish Americans]
I. Title.

E184.F5E53   973'.04'94541   77-73740
ISBN 0-8225-0229-1 [Library]
ISBN 0-8225-1027-8 [Paper]

International Standard Book Number: 0-8225-0229-1 Library Edition
International Standard Book Number: 0-8225-1027-8 Paper Edition

Library of Congress Catalog Card Number: 77-73740

2 3 4 5 6 7 8 9 10 85 84 83 82 81 80 79

. . . CONTENTS . . .

The land of Finland

PART I

The Land and the People
of Finland

Finland is a vast northern land of winter ice and snow, of summer midnight sun, and of water, forest, and rock. The unique landscape of this beautiful country has done much to shape the character of its people. Finland is a large nation—one of the largest in Europe. But with only 4.8 million inhabitants, it is at the same time one of the most sparsely populated. Finland is dotted with 100,000 sparkling lakes and winding waterways, edged by dense forests of pine and birch. In the north, much of it is wild country that does not easily lend itself to farming or to the building of cities. Finland is a country where there are miles and miles of land untouched by civilization—where a person can be truly alone with the natural elements.

1. *The Land*

The land itself was shaped during the last ice age, when all of northern Europe was covered with a massive layer of ice, miles deep. When the ice finally began to melt and retreated further north, it carved the rock beneath it and left behind thousands of lakes in the land that would become known as Suomi, or Finland. As the climate warmed and the land dried out, there appeared willow and dwarf birch trees, and finally great forests of fir and sprucc.

These elements of forest, water, and rock have been a part of Finland for thousands of years. And from the time that people settled in Finland, the trees and lakes have been an essential part of their way of life. The Finns have always used the forest wood to build their houses, to make their tools and toys—even their jewelry. In more recent times, they have been able to use the great network of waterways for travel and transport. Their deep spiritual love of nature and of solitude is reflected in their music, their poetry, and their artistic design. Even early Finnish religion was shaped by the natural elements. Who are these people who live in such harmony with nature, and where did they come from?

2. *The People*

The origins of the Finnish people have long been a subject for discussion. Throughout history, the Finns have become entangled in one identity crisis after another. In the ancient Icelandic sagas, or stories, Laplanders are called Finns and Finns, Laplanders, even though the two are completely different ethnic groups. Finns have also been called Swedes, Scandinavians, and even Russians.

The most persistant myth about Finnish origins was that started by a German anthropologist, Johann Friedrich Blumenbach. In his book *De Generis Humani Varietate Nativa*, published in 1775, Blumenbach divided all the world's people into five races, based on skin color. The Finns didn't fit into any of the five categories, so he lumped them in with the Mongols— the people of Asia. For a long time, scholars accepted this classification. Then research by anthropologists uncovered new evidence about the true ancestry of many of the world's people, including the Finns.

The first people to inhabit Finland were the Lapps, a race of northern hunters. But they were gradually pushed further north by new groups of people who arrived from neighboring lands.

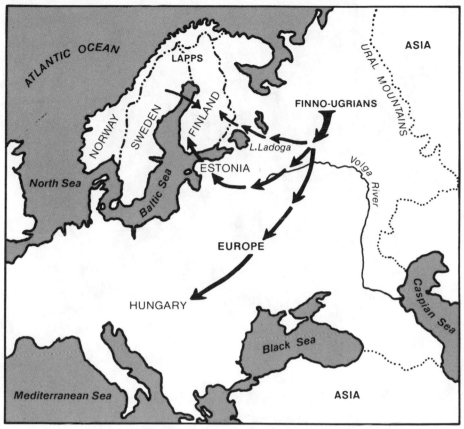

THE ORIGINS OF THE FINNISH PEOPLE

Scholars believe that about 2,000 years ago, a large group of tribal people—the Finno-Ugrians—left their homeland between the Ural Mountains and the Volga River in Russia and began wandering in search of a new place to live. Some of the tribes settled in what is now Estonia; some in Hungary. Two tribes, the Tavasts and the so-called "Proper Finns," crossed the Baltic Sea and settled in central Finland. Today the people who live in all these areas speak related languages, although they cannot understand one another in conversation.

The Karelians, another Finno-Ugrian tribe, came by land from the region of Lake Ladoga and made their homes in the area

9

From the earliest times, the people of Finland have
been skilled at making useful things out of wood.

north of modern Leningrad, Russia. From the west and south
came the Scandinavians, particularly the Swedes, who became
colonists and administrators in Finland after the country was
annexed by Sweden during the Middle Ages.

Finland's early settlers soon developed ways of coping with
their harsh environment. By the eighth century, they had begun
to perfect their own unique skills — skills their descendants would
bring to America many centuries later. Using handcrafted implements, they became expert foresters and builders, felling trees
and fitting interlocking logs into strong walls for their homes. They
roofed their dwellings with birchbark, and over it they laid turf to
keep out the cold. Since birchbark was available everywhere,
they used it for plates and platters. And in a manner similar to
that of the American Indians, they built sturdy birchbark canoes.

Because the long, hard winters and dense forests made communication difficult, most people in Finland kept to themselves in their own isolated settlements. It was this loose, disconnected political structure that made it relatively easy for Sweden to take over the country.

3. *A Duchy of Sweden*

During the 12th and 13th centuries, Sweden gradually conquered all of Finland. By 1362 the country had been made a duchy (province) of Sweden, and various Swedish noble families had set up their estates there. Although the language for conducting official business was Swedish, the majority of Finns continued to speak their own language. (Eventually Finland became a dual-language country.)

During this period, the relationship between the Swedes and the Finns was an agreeable one. Swedish administrators were sent to live in Finland, to provide political stability and a link with the Swedish throne. In return, the Swedes shielded Finland from attacks by German knights who enslaved the nearby Baltic states and from the fierce Tartars of the East. The Finns were allowed to play a role in the governing of their country and even had the right to send a delegation to Sweden's capital, to help elect a king. The countryside of Finland remained largely unchanged, and village life continued as it had for a thousand years. But things were not to remain the same forever: a dynamic young Swede was soon to make many changes in the Finnish way of life.

4. *Gustav Vasa*

In 1520, Christian II of Denmark invaded Sweden. In order to crush all opposition within the country, he ordered the massacre known to historians as the Stockholm Bloodbath. Nobles were slaughtered, churchmen hauled off to Denmark, and hostages dragged away in chains. Among the hostages was a young Swedish nobleman, Gustav Ericksson Vasa.

Gustav Vasa, king of
Sweden and Finland

Swashbuckling young Gustav soon made a daring escape and
returned to Sweden. In May 1520, he landed near Kalmar, where
he discovered that his sister and mother had been captured by
the Danes and that his father and his brother-in-law were dead.
Vowing revenge, he went from village to village encouraging
peasants to revolt against the Danes. By January 1521, when
news of his mischief reached the Danish king, the revolt was in
full swing.

Young Gustav began his campaign with no money or weapons.
But province after province came to his aid, and by June 1523,
the Danish king had been driven out of Sweden. Soon after,
Gustav Vasa was elected king. Founder of the Vasa line, he proclaimed a hereditary monarchy to prevent any further Danish
claims to the Swedish throne.

It was during Gustav Vasa's reign that Sweden broke with the Catholic Church. Seizing papal-held wealth and property on behalf of the Lutheran Reformation, Vasa proclaimed himself head of the Lutheran Church in Sweden and Finland. By the end of the century, the Lutheran faith had become generally accepted. In Finland, the coming of Lutheranism greatly helped the development of the Finnish language. This was because Lutheran services were conducted in the common language of the people rather than in the Latin of Roman Catholic services. In 1548, Michael Agricola, the bishop of the city of Turku, translated a Lutheran prayer book and the New Testament into Finnish. Agricola, who had earlier written a Finnish-language primer, has become known as the father of Finnish literature.

The title page from the New Testament translated by Michael Agricola in 1548

Generally, the Finns were treated fairly by the Swedes. But there were also disadvantages to life under Swedish rule. During the next 300 years, the Finns found that they had to fight and finance Sweden's constant wars with Russia and other countries. Russia and Sweden fought five wars, lasting more than 60 years altogether, between 1570 and 1809. Most of these battles were fought on Finnish soil and resulted in great destruction of crops and villages.

During the early 19th century, Finland, Russia, and Sweden, along with the rest of Europe, were caught up in the Napoleonic wars. In 1809, both Russia and Denmark attacked Sweden as a part of a plan devised by the French emperor Napoleon. Unable to hold out under this combined attack, Sweden was forced to sign a treaty giving Finland up to Russia. Finland was made a grand duchy of Russia and remained under Russian control until 1917, when the Bolshevik Revolution broke out and the czar was overthrown. The Finns took advantage of the confusion in Russia and declared their independence. Finland has been an independent republic ever since.

PART II

Finns along the Delaware

The first Finns in America came to set up a trading post at what is now Wilmington, Delaware. They left Gothenburg, Sweden, early in November 1637, and sailed to Holland in two small ships, *Kalmar Nyckel* and *Fogel Grip*. There, the ships were fitted out for a stormy three-month crossing of the Atlantic. They arrived at the mouth of the Delaware River in March 1638.

The expedition, led by Dutchman Peter Minuit, included 26 Finnish and Swedish crew members, some soldiers, and Minuit's Dutch aides. The group had no firm plans for permanent colonies such as those established by the English in Massachusetts and Virginia. For the Swedes and the Dutch, it was strictly a commercial venture.

At that time, Sweden was emerging as a new power in European politics, anxious to compete for markets and raw materials around the world. Peter Minuit, once director of the Dutch trading colony of New Netherland (now New York City),

This stamp was issued by the U.S. Postal Service in 1938 to commemorate the 300th anniversary of the settlement of New Sweden.

had first approached the Swedes about a New World venture. He had convinced a Finnish nobleman, a Swedish vice-admiral, and various private investors that grand profits could be made by operating the New Sweden Company in America. Materials could be obtained there for almost nothing, then sold to European buyers for a profit.

When they arrived in the New World, Minuit and his expedition laid claim to the west shore of the South Delaware River, between what is now Christina Creek, Delaware, and Trenton, New Jersey. As he had been instructed to do, Minuit purchased the land from the Indians. The immense tract of land, called "New Sweden," included parts of present-day Delaware, New Jersey, and Pennsylvania.

1. *Fort Christina*

To the nature-loving Finns, the new land was a paradise of thick forests, estuaries, and landlocked harbors. Game roamed the area, and the waterways teemed with fish. New Sweden seemed like a perfect place to settle. Soon the stillness of the forest was shattered by the sounds of ringing axes and falling timber as men began work on Fort Christina, named in honor of Sweden's child queen. They built a large fence of logs, and inside that, a log house for storing ammunition and the merchandise they would trade with the Susquehannock and Delaware Indians. They also built a large house in which all the settlers could live. Five hundred bricks brought from Stockholm were used for making a fireplace and oven. By July, the communal house was finished.

When Minuit and his party sailed away, they left behind a commander along with a few Swedes and Finns, and some Dutch soldiers. Those left behind began building three more log houses: one at Crane Hook to be used as a church, and the others to be used as homes. Minuit never saw the new buildings; he was killed in a shipwreck in the West Indies. After his death, two years were to pass before the first colonists arrived.

A monument at the site of Fort Christina, in Wilmington, Delaware, displays a model of the *Kalmar Nyckel*, one of the ships that brought the Finnish and Swedish settlers to the New World.

2. *Expeditions to New Sweden*

In the 17 years of Swedish control of the colony (from 1638 to 1655), 11 expeditions sailed for the New World. Although the settlers were Swedish subjects, about half were of Finnish origin. Many of the Finns were from families that had already left their homeland and had settled in Sweden. Their trek had actually begun about 60 years before in 1580, when the Swedish Crown had urged them to leave their homes in order to pioneer the wilderness land of west-central Sweden. The Crown had an ambitious plan in which some 12,000 to 13,000 Finns were offered homesteading land that would be tax-free for 10 years. In return, they hacked at the forests and turned the land into productive farms.

The traditional Finnish method of clearing land was simple. The Finns cut down trees and underbrush, usually in the autumn, and in the spring they set fire to the debris. This cleared the land for planting crops and provided wood ashes for fertilizer. It was a wasteful method, but accepted in those days when all of Sweden was covered with forests.

Then, in the 1630s, the situation changed. Valuable iron and copper deposits were discovered in Finnish-occupied lands. At the same time, the demand for wood increased. Swedes began complaining that the Finns were trespassing on their hunting grounds, and there were many fights over property rights. Finally, the Swedish government began outlawing the land-clearing practices of the "burnbeater Finns." Offenders were driven from their farms, jailed, or forced to leave the country. Those who offended a second time faced a death penalty.

Many "burnbeaters" were rounded up and herded aboard ships bound for the Delaware colony. Also put aboard were young men who had been jailed because they refused to fight any more of Sweden's wars in foreign lands. They were let out of jail and allowed to sail for New Sweden with their families. Some

A painting from 1883 picturing "burnbeater Finns" clearing the land

farmers and woodsmen who had accidentally failed to legalize their homestead rights also went along. They had decided that their last chance for property ownership was in the colony across the sea.

The voyage to New Sweden was a dangerous one. Expeditions were never properly planned, and often colonists set out in small bands aboard ships that were not very seaworthy, even for those days. They sailed without escort or protection from pirates and privateers, and some vessels never reached the new land. Supplies that the government promised to send sometimes failed to appear.

The 1640 expedition of 30 settlers, directed by Governor Peter Holland Ridder, did land safely. The Finns soon rejected the confining life inside Fort Christina, however, and left to establish their own settlements. Two such settlements were Finland, located between present-day Marcus Hook and Chester, Pennsylvania, and Uppland, where Chester now stands. They were the first permanent settlements in what later became the state of Pennsylvania.

Seventy Finns in the 1649 expedition were not so lucky. They were shipwrecked off the coast of Puerto Rico, imprisoned by the Spanish, freed, and then captured by the French at St. Croix and sold into slavery. Another group of about 100 Swedes and 250 Finns was attacked off the Canary Islands by three Turkish ships in 1654; their fate is unknown. Many Finnish refugees traveled via northern Norway, hoping to reach Holland, then America. One such group landed in New Amsterdam and never got to New Sweden at all.

Nevertheless, the Finns who survived the Atlantic crossing gradually swelled the population of the three little settlements. They had large, healthy families who pitched in to clear the land for their homes. It was this group of settlers who introduced to the New World what became known as the American log cabin.

2. *First Homes*

The Finns, with their long experience of life in the forests, were skilled in the art of building log houses. They used both round logs, with the bark intact, and dressed logs, or logs that had been smoothed and shaped. Their building methods were unique. In fact, it is the characteristic Finnish log cabin that has helped historians trace many of the original Finnish settlers whose family names were sometimes changed or shortened. The Finnish rail fence is another important clue in tracing Finnish ancestry.

The earliest homes along the Delaware River were one-room cabins hastily built of round, undressed logs by peasant farmers who had very few tools to work with. The doors fitted badly and

The historic Mortonson home near Philadelphia, Pennsylvania, is more than 300 years old.

the windows were simple, uneven openings covered with movable boards. Cracks and holes in the walls were filled with clay or moss. Chimneys were made of sticks covered with clay; the roofs were insulated with turf laid over tree limbs or rough planks. All the timbers were cut by hand, and the cabins were built without the use of a square or level. Yet despite their crude construction, they held up for many years. The Nothnagle house near Wilmington, which is standing today, was built by a Finn, Antti Niilonpoika, for a well-to-do Swede. It has lasted for 300 years. Unfortunately, except for those preserved as historical memorials, these cabins are becoming rare as more and more land is cleared for new buildings in the Delaware Valley.

One of these historic cabins was built in about 1655, at what is now Prospect Park, a few miles south of Philadelphia, Pennsylvania. The builder, Martti Marttinen, was from Rautalampi, Finland. When Marttinen reached Delaware in 1641, he soon simplified his name to Morton Mortonson. He was the great grandfather of John Morton, a member of the Continental Congress who cast the deciding vote in favor of the Declaration of Independence. Marttinen built his original cabin out of closely fitted oak logs. About 1698, a second log house was built close by for his son, Mathias, and his family. Later, the space in between the cabins was enclosed with walls of stone for added strength, and eventually a continuous roof covered the entire long, narrow structure. These ancient buildings have been restored and are now preserved as a memorial by the Pennsylvania Historical and Museum Commission. They are thought to be the oldest buildings in the state.

4. Colonial Life

As the settlers gradually improved their living conditions, they installed larger windows in their log houses. When bricks became available, they built fireplaces large enough so that outdoor ovens were no longer needed. And by 1655, everyone had a sauna.

The sauna, or Finnish bath, was an important part of Finnish life. In fact, it was almost as much of a necessity as food and shelter. The Finns believed that the "home spirit" dwelled in the sauna, and therefore since ancient times the sauna had been associated with birth, love, health, and death. No matter how humble the building, the sauna gave the Finnish settlers a sense of stability and a link with the past. For this reason, many settlers built and lived in their saunas before putting up their main cabins.

The typical immigrant sauna was a small log hut with one door, one window, and one airhole. The wood-burning *kiuas*, or stove, was made out of fist-sized stones that wouldn't crack from the heat. As the fire in the stove heated the stones, smoke poured into the sauna and out the airhole. When it got good and hot inside the sauna, the fire was allowed to go out, and the airhole was plugged with a cloth. The sauna was then ready for bathing.

A Finnish sauna

The bathers sat or lay on a platform built along the walls of the sauna, taking a "sweat-bath" in the hot air. Inside the little hut was a big pot of hot water. A barrel-sized tub of cold water also stood on the floor near the door. Lying on the platform or in the cold water tub were *vihta* — switches of cedar or birch branches — with which bathers beat themselves to stimulate circulation. After they had finished their sweat-baths, the bathers used stiff brushes and bars of home-made soap for lathering and scrubbing in the tubs of water.

Transplanted Finns carried many such customs and manners to the banks of the Delaware. Old skills inherited from their ancestors were put to steady use in the great forests of America. For example, Finns made almost everything they used out of wood. Plates, bowls, spoons, forks, ladles, and beer jugs with hinged lids and spouts were handcrafted with small *puukko* knives. They made their own sleighs, skis, boats, and wagons as they had done in their homeland. The familiar birchbark was made into baskets, boxes, sieves, and even containers for salt and pepper. The women braided grasses, reeds, and cord to make shoes, and cultivated flax, from which they wove intricately patterned linens.

Food was plentiful in the new settlement. Women made beer from persimmons, brandy from peaches, and wine from the native grapes. The traditional rye bread was baked and strung on a pole to harden over the fireplace, where it kept for weeks.

In all, New Sweden seems to have been a happy colony. It was small—probably no more than 400 people lived there at the time the Dutch took over in 1655. There were no slaves, and the settlers were friendly with the Indians from the beginning. The Finns, particularly those who headed for the backwoods, quickly learned the Indian languages. There is no evidence of protective stockades built by Finns in the backwoods; there seems to have been no need for them.

5. *Lasting Impressions*

In spite of neglect from the home country, political rivalries, and economic crises, the people of New Sweden made lasting contributions to their adopted land. They built the first flour mills, the first permanent homes, and the first roads in what are now Delaware and parts of Pennsylvania. At Fort Christina they established the first Lutheran church in America, with a Finnish clergyman, the Reverend Roerus Torkillus, as preacher. They mapped the regions in which they settled, set up the first organized government, and introduced both court and jury systems. It was the Finns and Swedes who prepared the way for William Penn, who arrived in 1682 to establish the colony of Pennsylvania. Penn was impressed with the Finns and Swedes; he admired their skill with the axe as well as their physical and moral strength. Penn wrote of the early settlers: "As they are People proper and strong of Body so they have fine Children, and almost every house full; rare to find one of them without 3 or 4 boys, and as many Girls; some six, seven and eight Sons: And I must do them that right. I see few Young men more sober and laborious . . ."

By the 1700s the Finns had begun to fade into the mainstream of American life. Distinctive characteristics and customs, as well as the use of the Finnish language, disappeared. At the close of the Revolutionary War, the new nation numbered three million English-speaking people. Minorities like the Finns and Swedes bent with the wind and became Americans alongside their neighbors.

One American of the period who left a lasting historical mark was John Hanson, great-grandson of a New Sweden colonist. He was elected president of the United States by the Continental Congress, an office he held for a year. Eight years later, in 1798, George Washington became president under the revised Constitution. Today, the four-lane highway between Annapolis, Maryland, and the District of Columbia is named for John Hanson.

PART III

Finns in Alaska

In 1727 Peter the Great, Czar of Russia, sent an expedition led by Vitus Bering to explore the area around Alaska. Peter, and later his widow, Catherine, hoped to set up a profitable fur trade in North America, as other European nations were doing.

Bering's second voyage in 1741 took him to the strait between Siberia and North America that now bears his name. In 1784, Russia took possession of Kodiak Island as a fishing and hunting base for the Russian-American Fur Company. Alexander Baranov, a former Siberian merchant, was made governor of the new territory. In the 1790s, Governor Baranov seized Sitka Island, from which the whole of Alaska was to be governed. The Sitka colony became a huge holding, stretching from Alaska almost as far south as present-day San Francisco.

Meanwhile, events that drastically affected Finland were taking place in Europe. In September 1809, Finland was taken over by Russia and was made a grand duchy, with the czar as grand duke. After this, many Finns began actively participating in the Russian-American Company in Alaska. Finnish sailors in Finnish-built vessels made the 13-month journey around Cape Horn, at the tip of South America. Some of the Finns who came to Alaska were political prisoners, sent from Siberia to do construction work. Others were employed in fairly high positions.

Governor Baranov ruled Sitka like a czar. He built an impressive governor's palace and furnished it with art treasures from St. Petersburg and a fine library of some 1,200 works in many languages. Vodka flowed freely at palace parties, to which Indian women were frequent visitors.

The island of Sitka in the mid-19th century

When Baranov died in 1818, he was succeeded by a series of governors of questionable ability and principles, for able administrators were not eager to settle in that remote outpost. Events in Finland, however, began to point toward better things in Alaska. Since Finland had high status as a self-governing grand duchy of Russia, gifted Finns could rise to important positions in the Russian government. Such was the case of Admiral Arvid Adolf Etholen, who served as governor-general of Sitka from 1840 to 1845. He sailed to Alaska with his wife and children aboard the Finnish-built ship *Nikolai* on September 12, 1839. Also aboard were 53 other settlers, including Pastor Uno Cygnaeus, who would serve a five-year assignment as Sitka's first Lutheran minister, and R. F. Sahlberg, a scientist and doctor who would serve for a year as a medical officer. Sahlberg's diary later provided a fascinating insight into the early life of the colony.

The *Nikolai* reached Sitka in the summer of 1840 after a perilous and stormy voyage around Cape Horn. Sahlberg wrote, "To be sure, the sleet and hailstones dampened the pleasure that being on deck brings, but one had to suffer this discomfort in order to see the wild seas. The waves rose high, higher than half-mast, and broke against the ship, threatening to engulf it completely."

Once there, the newcomers soon saw that life in the northern frontier post was wild and irresponsible. With a dizzy round of receptions, balls, drinking bouts, and card parties, homesick aristocrats did their best to recreate something of the "high life" of St. Petersburg. Many were hopelessly in debt for gambling. "God is high and the Czar is far away" was the standard response to criticism. "They have been in Sitka so long that they have abandoned all hope of getting home," Sahlberg wrote.

Although morals were low, profits were apparently high. The company carried on large-scale trading in furs and other goods, as well as fishing and panning for gold. Company-owned trading ships sailed to China, the Philippines, California, and Japan.

Governor Etholen and his wife began a massive program of reform, changing drastically the lives of company employees as well as native Alaskans. A 40-bed hospital, a public library, a playground, and a clubhouse for unmarried men were all built under their direction. Madame Etholen, a pious woman, made the altar linens for the new Lutheran chapel, and she and her husband donated a small pipe organ that was still used in the church during the 1880s.

The Etholens were particularly concerned about the exploitation of the native Alaskans. In 1841, the sale of liquor at all posts was banned. According to Sahlberg, "Some of the Russians wept at receiving the order." Fairs were begun at which native people could display their handiwork. The most lasting gift of Madame Etholen was her establishment of the first boarding school for native girls in Alaska. During their stay, the Etholens left a permanent mark on the area. Etholen Island, near Sitka, is named for these energetic and charitable people.

Admiral Arvid Adolf Etholen   **Madame Etholen**

Captain Hampus Furuhjelm, who became Sitka's 13th governor-general in 1858, was also a Finn. He first came to the territory with Admiral Putjatin's research expedition to the Arctic, where he christened two unknown islands in Possiet Bay, the Furuhjelm Islands.

When Alaska was sold to the United States in 1867, some Finns drifted south to Seattle and other mainland communities where they could find work. Many, however, stayed on and settled, particularly in Sitka, Juneau, Fairbanks, and Anchorage.

Though small in numbers, Alaskan Finns were, and are, proportionally well represented in government. William Alex Stolt, the Finnish consul in Anchorage, served as mayor of the city during World War II. Waino Hendrickson, the last acting governor of Alaska before it became a state, was born of Finnish parents. And Jalmar Kerttula, the majority leader of Alaska's senate, is of Finnish descent.

Finnish immigrants begin the long journey to the United States in 1893.
(Captain J. A. Rosquist, Helsinki City Museum)

PART IV

The Great Migrations

I'm going to America
Everyone is on his way.
The American shores are sanded
With gold they say.

I'll embark from Hankoniemi
On a small boat and go.
'Cause Finland can't support
The children of her poor.

Finnish immigrant ballad

Between the years 1864 and 1920, about 360,000 Finns set sail for America. They were part of what historians call the "new immigration"—a mass movement of people from Eastern, Central, and Southern Europe to American shores. Like immigrant Lithuanians, Poles, Slovaks, Greeks, and Russians, the Finns would provide manpower for America's expanding industrial economy. Most of the men headed for the mines and mills, the factories, the lumber camps and sawmills. Some became fishermen. Many of the women worked as domestics.

Although the literacy rate among Finns was about 80 percent higher than in other immigrant groups, few Finns could speak or write English. From the beginning, their most serious handicaps were problems with language and lack of industrial skills. As latecomers in American society, they generally had to take the most menial jobs.

The new immigrants did not quickly disappear into the American scene as the Finns did in Delaware in the 1630s and in Alaska in the mid-1800s. Their adjustment to American life was slow and often painful, though made somewhat easier by the lively community life that developed among Finnish-speaking Americans. Nevertheless, many of the more homesick immigrants soon wondered why in the world they had ever fallen victim to "America fever." About one-third of them eventually returned to Finland for good.

1. *Why They Left*

During the first half of the 19th century, a few Finns had crossed the seas to America, seeking fortune or opportunity in a new land. In the 1830s, a Finnish farmer named William Lundell had settled in the Fitchburg area of Massachusetts. At about the same time, Carl Sjökahl (Charles Linn) went to Alabama, then returned to Finland, where he recruited 53 workers. The women took jobs as maids in Montgomery and New Orleans, and the men worked on the railroad. During the gold rush of the 1840s, Finnish sailors who had gone ashore in California returned to Finland with pockets full of money. Inspired by the lure of gold, dozens of Finns followed seaman Edvard Kohn of Turku back to California. But beyond this handful of immigrants, very few people left Finland until after the American Civil War.

The real "America fever" began in Arctic Norway's Finnmark and Tromso provinces where, by 1865, some 6,000 Finns were working as fishermen, miners, and farmers. Life there was severe and dangerous, particularly for fishermen who sailed the stormy Arctic Ocean. "Few of the poor fishermen end their days in bed" was the old saying. They barely earned enough to exist, and they often spent what little money they had in the local saloon, fortifying themselves for their next gamble with death.

Farmers were not much better off. Northern Norway's poor peat soil, sudden frosts, and bitter cold made for sparse crops, and many farmers lived on the brink of starvation. Probably the unhealthiest jobs in the area were in the copper mines at

Kaafjord, where men faced bitter cold and the constant threat of accidents. But even these unpleasant jobs became less numerous during the 1860s. When they stopped altogether, many Finns were left with no place to go.

No wonder, then, that two agents from the Quincy Mining Company were so successful in recruiting Finns for work in northern Michigan's copper country. During the next 20 years, some 700 to 1,000 Finns came to the United States directly from Norway. Although their numbers were not great, their departure was greatly influential. Jobless people in Finland itself soon began to talk about America's need for miners; the news even carried to Russian Kola in Lapland, where 700 Finns lived. By the 1800s, some Finnish communities of only 200 had lost 30 of their inhabitants to "America fever."

Why did these Finns who loved their homeland leave for the land across the sea? Any number of reasons were given. Some were escaping unhappy love affairs; others wanted to get away from overbearing parents or persistent creditors. Some young men wanted to avoid serving in the Russian army, and some just wanted adventure in a far-off land. One father sent his son to America in the hope that the young man would forget his gypsy sweetheart. But the overwhelming reason for emigration was financial. "The heart pleaded 'no' but the stomach commanded 'yes'" was the saying during those hard days.

For the Finns, a way of life that had been unchanged for centuries was in great upheaval. In 1861, the Russian overlords issued an Imperial Decree that freed Finnish industry from strict regulation. At the same time, the government began chartering companies, organizing banks, and issuing currency. As a result, the lumber and sawmill industries boomed. Earlier Finnish society had been completely traditional, with families farming the same land for generations and living on what they produced. Now, people began to think in terms of jobs that paid money.

Farm families got rid of their traditional wooden utensils and homespun clothing, and replaced them with manufactured goods from the store. Farmers turned from grain crops to dairy products, which could be sold directly to sawmill communities. During winter, they worked at the mills for cash.

As small, scattered land holdings were combined into larger farm units, more and more people found themselves tenants instead of land owners. And the rapid growth of industry created a new and rootless labor force of seasonal workers who began moving to the cities in southern Finland, hoping to find work. Unfortunately, there simply weren't enough jobs to go around. Overpopulation in the industrialized areas set off a chain reaction that resulted in the horrible famine of 1866-1868.

The famine killed 107,000 more people than were born in that three-year period. In 1868, in one parish alone, 765 people

Finns receiving food at a charity dinner during the famine of the 1860s

starved to death while only 31 were born. People ate pine bark mixed with ground-up straw in feeble attempts to stay alive. The lucky ones existed on tough rye-flour bread and skimmed milk, or ate potatoes and salted cod and drank salt water. Under such appalling conditions, many Finns began to look toward America as a last chance of survival.

"America fever" first reached epidemic proportions in Oulu Province in northwestern Finland and spread south to Vasa, and eventually to urban areas such as Helsinki and Tampere. At first young, unmarried men left home; then, as time went on, girls left to work as servants or to become brides of Finns in America. Finally, whole families crossed the sea to the United States.

2. Disapproval at Home

As the emigration tide swelled, so did the cries of righteous indignation at home. People who stayed behind resented the loss of workers and of draft-age men. The clergy and the government officials with whom the emigrants registered for passports condemned those who left their home country for what were considered the evils and dangers of America. The officials did not seem to understand the economic pressures that forced poor people to look for a new life elsewhere. Instead, they insisted that there was plenty of work in Finland and that America was a sinkhole of vice, where so-called freedom led people to behave like "horses without bells."

A number of Finnish writers warned of the awful dangers and the low morals that emigrants would find in America. The new country was described as a "burial ground" where workers suffered from long hours, low pay, shameful diseases, drunkenness, loss of religious values, and persecution by big bosses. When those arguments didn't seem to work, they tried the "sour grapes" approach, saying that Finland was glad to get rid of the lower classes since they were nothing but trouble anyway.

The clergy and government officials claimed that many young husbands were abandoning their wives and children in order to satisfy their greed for American gold. In truth, however, records indicate that few of the men who left were married, and that those who were married went on ahead and saved enough money to send for their families in a year or so.

Finnish officials tried to discourage emigration as late as 1873, when the Finnish senate urged pastors of churches to issue warnings against it. At one point, the clergy even refused to recognize any marriage contracted by Finns in America. But nothing seemed to stop the flow of emigrants. In 1898, a senate committee declared that emigration could not be prohibited.

Looking back, it would seem that the only real defense against the "gospel of America" would have been jobs for the masses in the home country, along with suspended mail service to and from America. It was the letters sailing back across the Atlantic that gave Finns the courage to pack up and go. The letters told what season was best for traveling, where the jobs were, what living conditions were like, and where to find Finnish communities. Would-be emigrants were surprisingly well informed about seasonal economic conditions in America. When times were good, they came, but when there was a recession, they waited for better days.

3. "Gut Bai!"

Finland's hungry and jobless were convinced that once they reached America their money worries would be over. By paying 150 finnmarks (today worth about $50) for third-class tickets to the "fri kontri," they would soon be laughing about the old days when their sawmill wages were only two finnmarks a day.

During the 1870s and 1880s, most of these hopeful travelers left Finland via Sweden. But after 1883, when the Finnish Steamship Company was organized, they sailed directly from

The steamship *Urania*, carrying 509 passengers, prepares to leave Finland in 1893.

southern Finland's port of Hanko to England, and then on to America. Ships such as the *Sirius*, the *Urania*, the *Arcturus*, and the *Polaris* were well known throughout the country for their "first leg" transport. The port of Hanko was often crammed to overflowing with people who had no place to stay while they waited for their unscheduled departure. Up to 700 of them could be milling around at one time, talking, walking the streets, and clutching their meager belongings. The town had no accommodations for poor travelers, and usually every inch of floor space was spoken for. Often, crowds were stopped before they reached the port. They were told they must wait for several days before procceding to the docks, where they would have to wait again.

This watercolor painting by Emil Danielson shows Finnish immigrants boarding a ship in the port of Hanko.

Sometimes departures were emotional, but often they were marked with either forced gaiety or apparent indifference. One woman wrote, ". . . The emigrants marched on board—without a wet eye or a smothered sob. Will nothing move these people? Is it that they hide their feelings, or is it that they have none to conceal?" But there were those, particularly the older ones, who wept, knowing they might never see Finland again.

Once the emigrants reached Hull, in England, they boarded trains for the large port cities of Liverpool or Southampton. Most of them had never ridden fast trains before, let alone travel through a foreign land. The trip across the English countryside took them past fields of grazing sheep and pleasant farmers who waved cheerfully. The Finns responded, shouting in their best phonetics, "Gut bai!" But there were ominous signs too—the soot-blackened homes and buildings of the industrial towns. Could this be what people called "modern living"?

At the wharves, the Finns found themselves competing with all kinds of foreigners for cheap hotel lodging. They ate strange foods—tomatoes, for example—and sampled English biscuits with tea. Young men wasted their meager savings in saloons and dance halls, or on novelty souvenirs and junk jewelry. The girls bought fancy hats and corsets, symbols of the upper classes in the old country.

Sympathetic foreign observers were often shocked by the conditions that the emigrants had to endure. One Britisher described the scene at the Liverpool wharves, saying that "...the emigrants were collected like sheep..." whose "...passports, tickets, and goods were examined as though they belonged to beasts." By far their most treasured goods were the tickets, often sent by friends or relatives in America or paid for with borrowed money, and the addresses of Finnish contacts in the United States.

4. *The Atlantic Crossing*

The Finnish emigrants fared somewhat better than their English, Irish, and German predecessors who had crossed the Atlantic Ocean aboard American packet sail ships. Jammed in like cattle, the early emigrants had suffered terribly, and on some voyages, up to 10 percent of them had died.

Although conditions had improved by the time the Finns set out, they were still pretty grim. The Atlantic crossing usually took about 10 days, but storms and rough seas made the voyage seem like years. Passengers were crammed into poorly ventilated quarters with few sanitation facilities. People were violently sick, and the smell of vomit was unbearable. For those who *could* eat, rations of potatoes and herring were often cut short. In addition to physical discomfort, the emigrants had to endure the emotional shock of leaving friends, family, and country, perhaps forever. They bravely tried to remain cheerful by thinking about the trip's end.

39

5. *The "Fri Kontri"*

When they finally arrived in the new land, the immigrants' feelings were often mixed. Immigrants arriving in New York were thrilled by the Statue of Liberty, which symbolized a "land of hope, land of freedom." Those landing in other ports stared in awe at the high buildings and factory chimneys that belched black smoke.

Officials examined the newcomers for signs of illness and made sure that they had their disembarkation money. Since the recruiting of foreign workers by American companies was unlawful during some periods, Finns suspected of having prearranged jobs were turned back.

Interpreters were usually on hand to help Finns find temporary lodging in boarding houses or private homes, and to get them onto trains headed for their destination as soon as possible. This kindly volunteer service was a lifesaver to bewildered people who were suddenly thrust into the what one clergyman called the "beehive ..., [the] godless, cold hodgepodge of tongues...," of a strange city.

PART V

Settling Down

Two young Swedo-Finns, walking along a
New York sidewalk, spotted a half-dollar
lying in the gutter. One of them immediately bent down to pick it up but the
other kicked it into the center of the
street. 'We are not going to start that
small, now that we are in America. Leave
it alone!'

Anders Myhrman,
Finlands Svenskar i Amerika

Had most Finns chosen to come to America in 1800, they
would have shared the continent with only 5.7 million people.
A hundred years later, however, the population had increased to
81 million. Between the years 1840 and 1850, immigrants from
almost every European country came at the rate of 150,000 a
year, establishing themselves in good jobs and homesteading
choice property. The Irish stayed mainly in the cities, where many
of them helped to build railroads and canals. Most of the English
remained near seaports, while the Germans moved west to the
rich farmlands of Wisconsin and Missouri.

Competing for land and jobs with those who had settled before
them, Finnish-speaking Americans scattered in all directions.
Coincidentally, the land most of them chose—the northern lake
country of Minnesota, Michigan, and Wisconsin—resembled their
native land. By 1900, the majority of Finnish Americans were
living and working in the regions of these states bordering Lake
Superior.

1. *Jobs in the New Country*

Soon after they arrived, many of the Finns realized that they were hopelessly unprepared for the American job market. Few of them could speak English, and few had acquired any industrial skills. In his book *Finnish Immigrants in America*, A. William Hoglund described their plight thus: "Entering the mine and mill, men found few occasions to show their skills in horseshoeing, butchering and wood carving. Entering domestic employment, women found little occasion to show their skills in weaving, buttermaking and milking. . . ." In America, it was more important to learn to push an ore cart or open a tin can.

Finnish miners in Alabama, 1919

Miners

What jobs, then, were open to Finns whose chief qualifications were described by a newspaper reporter as those of being "...stiff-necked, having the strength of a bear, the endurance of a mule, and disciplined in the Old Country to perform even the most dismal jobs...."?

The answer: mining.

Thousands of Finns practically went straight from the trains coming from the port cities into the depths of the earth. For wages ranging from $30 to $50 a month, they dug copper in Upper Michigan, Montana, and Arizona; iron ore in Wisconsin, Minnesota, and Michigan; coal in Pennsylvania, Montana, Wyoming, and Washington; and gold or silver in South Dakota and Colorado.

Skilled and supervisory jobs in the mines were generally held by the English and other foreign-born workers who had come to the mining districts with previously acquired skills. The only Finns with mining experience were those few who had spent time in Norway; the others, unable to communicate in English, were assigned to the only most menial jobs.

Professor Matti Kaups of the University of Minnesota-Duluth describes the miserable working conditions in the mines: "Besides a physically taxing ten-hour day (six days a week) spent in the shaft mines, some of which reached to depths of more than 2,000 feet below ground level, the miners and laborers were exposed to hazards associated with mining. Particularly the use of explosives, falling rocks, and cave-ins of the hanging walls supported by timber resulted in injuries and death...." Ventilation was poor, sanitation was left to the hungry rats, and there was always a danger of fire in that strange, frightening world where "darkness was ruler and lord."

One newcomer described his first day in a Butte, Montana, mine: "I felt severe pains, and something like seasickness came over me, and my stomach emptied completely. Thereafter I felt a little better, but I was so weak that during the afternoon I was not able to do much more than push a cart of timbers and give my partner a little help in putting them into place. This was the way my first shift went. The second was easier, and by the third I began to feel like an old-timer. . . ."

In addition to enduring the physical hardships of mining, the new Finnish-Americans had to cope with the rigid organization of the mining companies, which was completely different from the family-oriented farm life they had always known. The mining companies set up the jobs, the pay, and the working hours, and that was that. There were no festivals, no "blue Mondays," and no "nonsense" about personal problems. Workers who couldn't stand the strange new industrial discipline were fired. Companies were interested only in how much their employees produced— not in how they felt.

The Finns also had to face the anti-Finnish feeling that often sprang up among their co-workers of other nationalities. Some hostility arose because of the Finns' over-eagerness on the job. Then, too, Finns had a reputation for being trouble makers, because they had led dozens of wildcat strikes to protest exploitation by big bosses in the Michigan and Minnesota mines.

In spite of all their problems, those Finnish miners who kept working at it did well in their pursuit of the "almighty dollar." They loved adding up their money on payday and figuring what it would be in finnmarks. Sometimes it was as much as a clergyman would make in the Old Country.

Lumberjacks

Rather than learn the new tasks required of them in the mines, many Finnish immigrants found jobs that made use of their woodsmen's skills. They had earned a reputation as excellent woodsmen—strong, tough, and able to endure the rigors of

A Finnish lumberjack in northern Michigan drives a sledge loaded with logs.

working the northern forests in the severe winter cold. Thousands found jobs in logging camps scattered across the country from Maine to Washington, and along the Oregon and California coast. But logging was back-breaking labor. There were no bulldozers and trucks to do heavy work, so Finnish teamsters hauled the logs to water with the help of teams of horses. The teamsters shivered at the rollways on the banks of rivers and lakes as rafting crews, working in waist-deep, freezing water, floated logs out to the rafts that carried them downstream to the mills.

There were other lumbering jobs that were not quite so strenuous. Men who were too old to pull a crosscut saw were called "soupbones," and were given odd jobs such as cooking or filling the woodboxes. Others, the "road monkeys," sanded the icy hills or cleaned up after the horses.

Living quarters in the lumber camps were miserable. Inside the huge, drafty, foul-smelling bunkhouses, cots were often so close together that there was no room to walk between them.

A bunkhouse with "muzzle-loader" bunks

Men climbed into these "muzzle-loader" bunks from the ends.
The mattresses, filled with hay or straw, were usually crawling
with bedbugs and lice. Married men who came home on weekends de-loused themselves in the sauna, using the simple exter-
mination method of hanging their clothes on a pole over the
steaming rocks of the *kiuas*. Although the ethnic slur of the day
was "dirty Finns," these workers were far from that. Only their
work was dirty; all traces of filth disappeared in the sauna, along
with the suds of their harsh yellow laundry soap.

Finnish loggers earned a reputation for tough, drunken fighting, particularly when they came out of the woods after a long
winter with the season's pay—sometimes as much as $500—
bulging in their pockets. In California, those working in the red-
wood forests often joined their equally rowdy countrymen, the
sailors of the "Finnish navy" who worked on the lumber
schooners along the coast.

46

Lumbering and mining lured thousands of Finns to Minnesota. The first group settled in Red Wing in 1864, but a severe epidemic of cholera killed many of them. Those who survived decided that the unfamiliar open fields and hardwood groves of Goodhue County were not for them, so they moved north or west. By 1930, there were 60,000 Finns in Minnesota. Today, many counties of that state still have large Finnish populations.

Other Workers

Of course, not all of the Finns who came to America worked in the mines and forests. There were jobs to be had in other industries as well, though the pay was not always as high as that in mining or lumber.

In the harbors of the Great Lakes, Finns worked at loading and unloading ore boats. They did hard, heavy work for very little pay. In 1899, an ore shoveler earned 10 cents a ton. To shovel one ton of ore, a worker had to lift 6,250 shovelsfull, each weighing 20 pounds. Those who worked in the stone quarries of New England, California, and the Midwest worked just as hard and earned just as little.

Earning a living as a fisherman was equally difficult. By 1897, about 2,000 Finns were living in Astoria, Oregon, and fishing for salmon in the Columbia River. But the weather was undependable, and so were the salmon catches. In the 1890s, a man had to haul a ton of fish to make $80. Not only was the pay low, but fishing was also dangerous work. In 1906 alone, 78 Finnish fishermen lost their lives. Jobs were spotty and seasonal, and relief programs and unemployment compensation did not exist. During labor strikes or lay-offs, many fishermen tried their luck in Alaska.

Other Finns joined railroad crews and laid tracks for the Ashtabula-Youngstown & Pittsburgh Railroad, the Northern Pacific, the Duluth-South Shore & Atlantic, and the Duluth-

Mesabi & Iron Range Railroads. North of the border, Finns worked on the Canadian-Pacific Railroad, which eventually reached to British Columbia.

A number of other Finns found jobs in the factories and mills of New England, especially in Massachusetts. Their hard-working, thrifty ways brought favorable comments from observers who noted their similarity to solid New Englanders. Elsewhere, the steel mills in Pennsylvania, Ohio, and West Virginia attracted many job-seekers, as did the wire-manufacturing plants in Illinois.

Many Finnish immigrants looked for work in large American cities. By 1920, 19,000 foreign-born Finns were living in eight major cities: Boston, New York, Cleveland, Detroit, Chicago, Minneapolis, Los Angeles, and San Francisco. These "city Finns"

A Finnish-owned printing business in Calumet, Michigan

worked mainly as tailors, goldsmiths, silversmiths, watchmakers, carpenters, and masons. Many Finnish women and girls, brought up in a world of clean houses and immaculate kitchens, found jobs as domestics. In 1918, the magazine *Nation* reported that "...the Finnish servant is one of the most sought for and best-paid on account of her nature, intelligence and efficiency."

2. *Back to the Land*

Finns seldom stayed put in their first jobs; they searched endlessly for a better life, a better position, and a kinder employer. And as time went on, they became increasingly frustrated with industrial life, factory whistles, and arrogant bosses; with saloons and drunken fights in the soot-blackened towns. Strikes, lay-offs, and low pay all seemed to remind them of the old proverb "oma tupa, oma lupa," which means "when one has his own place, he is his own boss." Many Finns had come to America because they could not afford to own land back in Finland. Ownership of land had become to them a symbol of prosperity and independence.

The Homesteaders

By the early 1900s, miners from Minnesota's Iron Range were spending more and more time in the northern wilderness, clearing small patches of land they could call their own. During weekends, strikes and lay-offs, they gathered friends and family members and headed for small holdings of cut-over stumps and brush they had bought for next to nothing. Some Finns in upper Michigan worked at the mines only between potato crops, just long enough to earn some necessary cash for their farms. Even in Wyoming, coal miners found valleys in which to farm.

A 1907 strike in the Minnesota mines sent thousands of miners to homestead lands. And in Michigan during the copper strike of 1913-1914, thousands more headed for cheap stump lands

Finnish farmers in Wisconsin stand beside a
pile of rocks they have cleared from their land.

where fires still smouldered from the lumber companies' massive
sweeps.

Such cheap land was not only poor, it was remote. It was the
land where the trails ended. The crude roads were miles away,
and the silence of the vast wilderness was broken only by the
sounds of forest animals and birds. Bachelor Finns settling in
these lonely regions came to be known as hermits.

Since power tools were unknown and there was often no
money with which to buy dynamite, settlers removed stumps
with axes and grub hoes. Whole families worked to fell and burn
old trees and fill the stump holes. When plowing time came, they
hitched up a team, forced their plows into the earth, and literally
bounced from rock to rock. Out in Washington state, the stumps
were particularly hard to remove because they were of old ever-
green trees surrounded by huge growths of underbrush. In the
Dakotas, settlers fought sudden rain storms, blizzards, and
crop-scorching summer droughts in their efforts to farm their
homesteads.

50

But somehow they did it. Their jack-of-all-trades skills helped them to clear land and construct farm buildings. A New Englander said of them: "Every good Finnish farmer can turn his hand to anything, from making furniture to making shoes. . . ."

Most Americans thought the land that the Finns settled was impossible to farm. A reporter for the *Sunday Mining Gazette* of Houghton, Michigan, wrote that the Finnish immigrant took cutover land when nobody else in the world had the courage to tackle it and ". . . turned that worthless stumpage into mighty valuable farm land." The director of Minnesota's Northeast Experimental Station wrote: "Of all racial stocks, the Finns have created wealth where none existed before in greater measure and degree than any other." And a *New York Times* reporter observed that the Finns in the Lake Superior region were taking a land of charred stumps and "creating a paradise."

A homestead on cutover land in Michigan

Young Finnish immigrants seated in front of
their log house in Rock, Minnesota, 1914.

The Finnish homesteaders had to build homes as well as clear
their land. So together, families and friends built their saunas and
lived in them until they could put up the main houses. They built
many other distinctive structures. A typical Finnish building was
the hay-drying barn, built out in the fields. It was purposely made
with air spaces between the logs so that the air could circulate
through the hay and dry it out thoroughly. When the hay was
dry, it was hauled to the cattle barn in the farm yard.

Finns homesteading along the borders of the rocky area known
as the Canadian Shield, about 100 miles north of Minneapolis and
St. Paul, used pine and poplar logs for their buildings. Their tools
were simple: a saw, two kinds of axes—a broad axe for hewing,
and an ordinary double-bitted axe for chopping—a plumbline,
and an auger. They used stone and mortar to build chimneys, and
greased paper (or glass if they could afford it) for windows.
Although none of the immigrants were professional builders,

they were usually able to construct a livable cabin within a few days. Often, friends or family members who were skilled carpenters or cabinetmakers helped to put on the finishing touches.

One fine example of a Finnish-American homestead farm is the Musakka home in St. Louis County, Minnesota. Built around 1910 by an immigrant from Viipuri, Finland, it has been abandoned for 30 years, but still stands, as sturdy as when it was first built.

By 1920, over half the Finnish population in the Lake Superior region had left the mines and camps to settle in such homemade log structures. Minnesota alone had 4,700 Finnish farms, most of which were adjacent to the Vermilion and Mesabi iron-bearing mountain ranges in St. Louis County.

The Finnish Farm Woman

One of the strongest forces in making homesteading a success was the Finnish farm woman. It was she who held things together in the home and community while her husband was in the mines, forests, or fields. And it was she with her incredible energy and wide range of skills who made survival in the wilderness possible. In his book *The Finns in America*, John I. Kolehmainen cites the example of a Toivola, Michigan, woman—one of thousands who took it all in stride. "She bore thirteen children, ten growing to adulthood; for forty years she was the region's only midwife, making 103 safe deliveries. When her husband worked at distant logging camps, she took charge of the farm; she hitched the horse, plowed and harrowed, sowed seed by hand from a dishpan; she milked the cows and nursed the ailing stock. She tanned hides and made footwear, spun wool and knitted garments. She hauled food supplies from the nearest store, a round-trip journey requiring three days. She kept the farmhouse in repair, raised the chimney, and found time to help the neighbors; once she rescued a child from a 28-foot well. She felt no sense of being a

The immigrant women who homesteaded in the American wilderness inherited their skills and their energy from their hard-working Finnish ancestors.

heroine, wrote a reporter, but because she had versatile ability and unquenchable energy, she lived up to the standards of that day. These people had to work hard, do those things, or go under."

But many women paid dearly for the chance to live on their own land and bring up their children on those remote farms. Lonely, fearful, and tired, young women became old long before their time. Many had only their Bibles for comfort.

Otto Walta, Folk Hero

The heroes in American folk tales are usually people from simple backgrounds who use their native intelligence and cunning to outwit the city slickers. The Finns in Minnesota had their own resourceful folk hero, Otto Walta. A kind of Paul Bunyan figure, Otto Walta was reputed to be six-foot-four and to weigh at least 240 pounds. "Hard as nails," people said. "Tough as a bull moose." He was so strong that he could rip good-sized trees out of the ground and carry huge boulders as though they were armloads of feathers. Some yarn-spinners swore he could bend a three-inch steel bar into the shape of a fish hook. And eat? Why, he could devour several loaves of bread and drain a bucket of milk in a single gulp.

During plowing time, when most people struggled to plow the rocky, rutted ground, Otto decided he could do the job better than any horse. He fixed up a pair of old shoes with hooks jutting down from the toes, harnessed himself, gave the reins to his brother, and proceeded to plow his land.

Once Otto Walta won a big argument with the railroads. The huge Finn wanted to speed up clearing land on his homestead, but didn't like to work his animals and couldn't afford dynamite. So he hiked three miles across the swamp to the railroad tracks, ripped up an 800-pound rail, and carried it home. It made a fine crowbar for prying out stumps. Folks said that the stumps "came out of the ground just like potatoes."

One day some railroad people came looking for their missing rail, and asked Otto who had helped him haul it to his farm. "Nobody," said Otto, but they didn't believe him until he hoisted it to his shoulder and walked around with it as if it were a broom handle. The railroad men looked at each other and did some figuring. It would take a whole crew of men to build a road across the swamp to Otto's farm, and another whole crew to haul the rail back along the road to the tracks. They walked off, defeated; it would be cheaper to let Otto keep the rail.

Although stories about Otto Walta were exaggerated, he was indeed a real person. The real Otto was eccentric and strong, and he did have a mysterious past. He was born in Pomarkku, Finland, in 1875, one of nine children of Lauri and Sofia Kulmala. When he came to America in the late 1890s, he brought with him his reputation for feats of strength in contests and for fights with

Otto Walta (left) and two of his brothers

knives and fists. Some said he had probably accidentally killed someone in a fight, and that's why he had changed his name to Walta. At any rate, after a stint in the mines at Hanna, Wyoming, he wound up in northern Minnesota in about 1911.

Michael Karni, a specialist in Finnish-American culture at the University of Minnesota, explains the big Finn's popularity as a folk hero. Otto, he says, fit the pattern of many Finns who felt guilty about leaving their home country—who felt that they had abandoned their native land and people. To compensate for having left, Otto Walta stayed as "Finnish" as possible, never learning English and refusing to adopt the American attitude toward work. He talked about going back to Finland but never did. Yet he remained alienated from American society all his life. As a folk hero, Otto did easily what for others was a struggle; he plowed his own ground, cleared his own stumps, and never had to worry about payments on farm implements.

Few people remember Otto Walta anymore. He was a hero at a special time, and the life that his contemporaries lived has changed. Most of the homesteads are abandoned now. Children and grandchildren of the original builders prefer scrambling for a living in the cities to grubbing for an existence under harsh conditions in the country. Some descendants have auctioned off the family farms; others use them only for hunting and fishing camps. Perhaps, someday, those farms will be settled again in another back-to-the-land movement.

3. *Banding Together*

Because they were latecomers, often lacking in industrial skills and the ability to speak English, the Finnish immigrants of the late 1800s and early 1900s did not blend quickly into the American scene. Their adjustment to American life was slow and often painful, but they had many resources to help ease the way.

Family Life

Finns are traditionally devoted to their families, and the immigrants brought this tradition with them to America. Their life at home centered mainly around the kitchen and the sauna. In the kitchen there were always the reassuring smells of homemade rye bread and cardamom coffee bread baking. Finnish housewives made *mojakka*, a fish and potato chowder, and *kalakukka*, a pie made from bread dough with white fish inside. *Uunijuusto*, a special custard, was made with the first milk from a cow after she had calved. The Finnish smorgasbord, soup bubbling on the stove in heavy iron pots, and dishes of herring or salmon all meant hospitality, Finnish style.

The sauna was another part of the Finnish home that served as a center of family life. The sauna and the traditions associated with it gave the Finns stability and a link with the past that was almost as necessary as food or shelter. The Finns went to their saunas after a day of exhausting labor. There they sweated out their weariness along with the grime and came out refreshed and relaxed. In the absence of medical specialists and Medicare, they treated their rheumatism, arthritis, colds, and flu in the sauna. Sometimes mothers gave birth to their babies there because it was clean, warm, and private, and there was plenty of hot water handy.

For the children of Finnish immigrants, life was often difficult. But as adults, many of them now recall their childhoods fondly and feel that they had richer, better lives in those days than children do today.

During the 1920s, many of those children who lived in western rural areas went to school in one-room cabins, built of hand-hewn timbers. Many schools could be reached only by country roads that were little more than wagon tracks. Gray, grim, and forbidding on the outside, the schools were usually warm and cheery inside, with their box stoves glowing red-hot to counter the 40-below-zero temperatures. Some teachers in lumbering and farming communities had no more than an eighth grade education themselves; most were fresh out of high school. But they were equal to the task of teaching young Finns to speak English, to read and write, and to learn their numbers.

Finnish children usually skiied to school in winter, sometimes over a distance of three or four miles, carrying their lunches in a canvas bag over their shoulders. When they walked, they toted their lunches of salted herring, a couple of slices of homemade bread, milk in jars, and sometimes an apple—all wrapped by their mothers in a Finnish-language newspaper and stuffed into an empty lard or coffee pail.

A schoolhouse for Finnish children in Brimsom, Minnesota, built in 1908

Community Life

Immigrant Finns soon realized that an effective way of easing life's difficulties in America was to band together as a community. Collective action, they believed, would change the new country into the land they had dreamed of. They reasoned that leisure time should be used for good purpose—to educate themselves and their children, and to keep Finnish culture alive.

As a result, all Finnish communities had political organizations, gymnastic societies, fraternal orders, glee clubs, and mixed choruses. There were all sorts of activities, which today would be called "enrichment programs." Violin, piano, and mandolin recitals were scheduled, along with readings, speeches, bazaars, debates, and dramas. Sewing circles and reading-study groups flourished, as did publishing associations. The publishing network established by various Finnish-American groups were so

59

successful that in the 1920s, each Finnish household subscribed to an average of three Finnish-language publications.

One community that helped to set the trend toward organized community activities was the mining town of Calumet, Michigan. The Finns called Calumet *pesapaikka*, or nesting place, and it was here that they established a number of Finnish-American institutions that had lasting importance. By 1900, there existed in Calumet the Apostolic-Lutheran Church, the Saturday and Summer School, the Evangelical Lutheran Church, and the Calumet Finnish Mutual Aid Society. There was also a literary society, a printing company, a book company, a lending library, a land company, and a weekly newspaper, *Amerikan Suomalainen*, or "The American Finnish Journal." Also of great importance was the Temperance Society, patterned after the Norwegian Good Templar organizations.

Finnish communities that followed the example of Calumet were often willing to spend a lot of money to keep their organizations active. Since each organization wanted its own building for a particular purpose, some communities maintained several community buildings, often worth thousands of dollars each. "Finn halls" soon became landmarks wherever Finns lived in large numbers.

Cooperatives

Perhaps the most effective and practical community organization the Finns developed in America was the consumer cooperative, or co-op. Today, the idea of the consumer cooperative sounds sensible and down-to-earth. Organizations owned and operated by and for the benefit of participating members are great ways to stretch household income. But when the immigrant Finns organized their cooperatives, the idea was an ethnic curiosity—different, and maybe a bit dangerous. "The Finns brought in the co-ops. To the Finns, let the co-ops belong," commented skeptics. One American said, "Those Finns have consumer co-ops for everything from baby shoes to coffins." And this was just about the case.

The need for co-ops was basically economic. People wanted to save money on things they needed to buy. At the same time, they wanted to shop in places they could call their own, where they could conduct their business in Finnish. Some co-ops began as buying clubs where people pooled their money in order to buy goods in large quantities at reduced prices.

By 1916, the Finns were running about 70 cooperatives in the United States, most of which were general stores. Twelve of the larger ones reported a combined business of $450,000 a year — a whopping amount in those days. Unhappily, however, a number of co-ops ran into financial trouble because the people hired to run them lacked business training and experience.

Merchandise displayed in the window of a co-op store in Wisconsin

In 1917, delegates from 19 cooperatives in the Midwest organized the Cooperative Central Exchange in Superior, Wisconsin. Three years later, this wholesale organization's sales to 31 Finnish co-op members totaled $409,591. In 1963, shortly before its merger with Midland Cooperatives, Inc., its sales to 242 cooperatives, 90 of which were begun by Finns, totaled $21.7 million. Americans decided that *this* was more like it.

By 1943, Americans' attitudes had changed so much that about half the co-op members served by the Superior exchange in

This building was acquired by the Cooperative Central Exchange in 1918, one year after its establishment. In 1931, the name of the organization was changed to Central Co-operative Wholesale.

Michigan, Wisconsin, and Minnesota were non-Finnish. This general trend was evident in almost all communities where co-ops flourished. At the same time, English was replacing Finnish as the language for conducting business in the co-ops. An employee remarked: "There are two hard nuts to crack—to teach English to a Finlander, and Cooperation to an American." The Finnish language died hard, however, and it wasn't until the 1950s that English replaced Finnish in the co-ops at virtually all levels. "Now," complained an oldtimer, "we have to take an interpreter to our own store!"

According to Michael Karni of the University of Minnesota, the co-op movement was an important unifier in Finnish-American society. A co-op store was the one neutral territory in which all Finns could meet and work together.

In recent years, co-ops have made a triumphant return in the form of huge and powerful credit unions, buying services, food chains, travel clubs, department stores, banks, and many other organizations. An example of this is the Greenbelt Consumer Services in Silver Spring, Maryland. It is one of the nation's oldest and largest co-ops, with more than 38,000 member families. Greenbelt's furniture division, *SCAN*, buys much of its merchandise from two or three co-ops in Finland for sale in America.

The Finns' consumer cooperative isn't considered odd anymore. When it began, it was just ahead of its time.

4. *Divisions within the Community*

With their cooperatives and community organizations, Finns impressed outsiders as being a tightly knit, clannish bunch. They stuck to their language and customs, married within their own community, and stubbornly guarded themselves against too much interference from strangers. Often they lived in their own part of town or in settlements that became copies of those back in Finland.

In reality, however, all Finns did not think alike on every issue. Finns are by nature individualists rather than mass followers, and once the immigrants became used to the new freedom of America, they began to find ways to express their varied social and religious convictions. The groups that they formed were usually at odds with each other for one reason or another, and at times they were openly hostile.

Most of the immigrants fitted themselves into one of several factions: the "Church Finns," the "Temperance" or "Dry Finns," whose participants were usually Church Finns, and the "Labor Finns," socialists who generally stayed away from formal religious activities. And because of the Finnish fondness for being leaders rather than followers, there were splinter groups within the major factions, along with rebels, hard-liners, peacemakers, and those who couldn't agree with anyone. All appear to have been stormy in nature and outspoken in their beliefs.

Religious Groups

In America, the Finns found that they were not forced to belong to any church or to pay taxes in order to maintain their church status as they had been in Finland. Even so, more than 25 percent of the immigrants worked for and developed churches of their choice.

The first arrivals in Michigan's copper country were members of a Finnish religious group called the Laestadians, named for the powerful revival preacher L. L. Laestadius. This group had some unorthodox religious beliefs, among them that the ministers of the church did not have to be ordained and that each individual church congregation had the right to rule itself. At first the Laestadians joined with other Scandinavian Lutherans in Michigan, but later they separated from the Norwegians and Swedes and formed their own association. By 1884, 22 lay preachers were serving the loosely organized religious bodies of Laestadians, or

The Apostolic Lutheran Church in Laurium, Michigan, around 1925

Apostolic Lutherans, a name coined in Calumet, Michigan. Still in existence today, the Apostolic Lutherans have now split into at least four different groups and apparently have no plans for merging with any other American Lutheran church.

Many Finnish immigrants were not interested in the unorthodox brand of religion practiced by the Apostolic Lutherans. They wanted to continue religious life in the spirit and style of the Church of Finland. The first pastor from the Church of Finland, Alfred E. Backman, arrived in Calumet, Michigan, in 1876. He served for seven years before he returned to Finland because of ill health.

Ordained ministers from Finland generally had a hard time of it in the United States. None were prepared for the moral decay they found in rough mining and lumbering communities. They were also discouraged by language problems, by the Americanization of the church, and by the religious indifference and resentment of the clergy that were common among the late 19th century immigrants. These energetic ministers were badly overworked; in 10 years, one hardworking cleric traveled 84,560 miles, gave 1,533 sermons, and conducted 769 worship services. Of the 63 Church of Finland ministers who served in the United States before 1925, about 40 returned to the home country.

It was clear from the beginning that trying to transfer the doctrine of the Church of Finland to America unchanged would not work, nor would control by the mother church be acceptable. But it was also clear that trained pastoral leadership and parish education were greatly needed in the United States. In 1885, Pastor J. K. Nikander arrived from Finland with what became the solution to the problem. He was instrumental in the founding of the Finnish Evangelical Lutheran Church of America, or the

Pastor J. K. Nikander

Suomi Synod. Furthermore, he established a college and seminary in Hancock, Michigan, to provide religious education for the new church. The Suomi Seminary educated 119 pastors from its opening in 1904 until 1958, when it became a part of the Lutheran School of Theology in Chicago. Today, Suomi College continues to function as a privately supported junior college for liberal arts, vocational and social programs, and courses in religion.

Another Finnish church, the Finnish-American National Evangelical Lutheran Church, had been organized in 1898 to provide an alternative to the Suomi Synod. The National Lutherans emphasized the role of the people in governing the church and the importance of the Gospel. In 1964, this group became affiliated with the conservative body of Lutheran churches known as the Missouri Synod. Two years earlier, the Suomi Synod had shared in the founding of another affiliation of Lutheran churches, the Lutheran Church of America.

Social Reform Groups

In addition to forming religious groups, the Finnish immigrants joined together to fight for social and political causes. The "Temperance" or "Dry Finns" came into existence in response to drinking problems among Finnish immigrants.

Drunkenness was a dangerous pitfall for many immigrant men, particularly those who were unmarried. According to temperance journals, hundreds of saloons run by Finns and other immigrants parted bored, thirsty miners and loggers from their wages at the rate of about $6.5 million a year. And the Finns were the first to agree that alcohol brought out the worst in them.

A number of local abstinence societies appeared in the mid-1800s, but the first big blow against the "demon rum" was the Finnish National Temperance Brotherhood, organized in 1889. By 1909, membership rolls boasted an impressive 7,057. In 1919,

Members of the Finnish National Temperance
Brotherhood in Eveleth, Minnesota, 1904

Finns joined with other American prohibitionists in celebrating the passage of the Eighteenth Amendment, which prohibited the sale of alcoholic beverages.

Another organization formed by Finnish immigrants was the social reform group called the "Labor Finns." This group was started by refugee radicals who fled Finland from 1899 to 1905, the years during which the Russians tried to force the Finns to accept Russian culture and government. By 1906, the radicals had organized a national Finnish Socialist Federation. They built a successful and powerful socialist organization in America, and then ruined it by arguing over issues of industrial unionism and, later, communism. By 1913, there were 13,847 members of the far leftist groups. Their activities were cultural and social as well as political.

Finnish socialists did establish several newspapers: *Raivaaja* in Fitchburg, Massachusetts; *Tyomies* in Hancock, Michigan; *Industrialisti* of Duluth, Minnesota; *Naisten Viiri* of Superior, Wisconsin; *Toveri* in Astoria, Oregon; and *Vapaus* in Sudbury, Canada.

There is little doubt that the early Finnish socialists and unionists contributed greatly to America's social consciousness. They braved the wrath of the "Establishment" long before it became fashionable to do so.

Workers make up the pages of *Tyomies*, a socialist newspaper established in 1903 and still published in 1977. The Finnish-language paper appears once a week and has about 2,000 subscribers.

PART VI

The Swedish-Speaking Finns

During the 1800s and early 1900s, immigration authorities and census takers had all sorts of unique ways of categorizing Finns. Some decided that everybody born in Finland was a Finn; others maintained that since Finland was a grand duchy of Russia, those Finns traveling with a Russian passport were Russian. A number of Finns who left from ports in Sweden and Norway wound up on those countries' lists, while Finns moving to Canada from the United States were considered Americans. A favorite system, particularly in Canada, was to classify everybody by mother tongue. Thus, the many people who had been born in Finland but brought up to speak nothing but Swedish were often classified as Swedes.

After about 1910, word sifted through that about one-fifth of the so-called Swedes were actually Finns, but by that time the damage had already been done. The impact of these early mistakes was later felt when the quota system came into effect in the United States during the 1920s. Under that system, only three percent of the number of Finns already in the United States in 1890 could be admitted each year. Once the quota was filled, the gates were closed until the following year. With such a small number of immigrants classified as Finns, three percent didn't amount to much, so fewer Finns were allowed to enter the country. This was one of the reasons why, during the 1920s, many Finns emigrated to Canada and Australia, where no such rules applied.

Most of the Swedish-speaking Finns (those labeled as Swedes) were from the southwest and coastal communities of Finland, and from Ostrobothnia. Their reasons for emigrating were like those of other Europeans. They wanted jobs, land, adventure, and a chance for a new life.

By 1870, a number of Swedish-speaking Finns had settled in New York City and in Ludington, Michigan. During the 1880s, more came to New York City, to Worchester, Massachusetts, and to southern Michigan. By the time of World War I, there were clusters of Swedish-speaking Finns in Pennsylvania, New York, Michigan, Minnesota, Wisconsin, Illinois, and the Rocky Mountain states, as well as in Canada. By far the greatest number settled in Washington state.

Swedish-speaking Finns at a logging camp in Washington

The Swedo-Finns were generally good businessmen. They opened small shops and bakeries, worked as watchmakers and locksmiths, and started insurance companies, timber companies, and sawmills. Some of the businesses were conventional ones, while others took the co-op route.

One example of a successful co-op established by Swedo-Finns was the Olympia Veneer Company of Washington, which became one of the biggest veneer-producing companies in the United States. It began soon after World War I, at a time when salaries and working conditions in the Puget Sound area were grim for people in the woodworking industry. Edward Westman, Axel Erikson, and J. Lucas got together 125 people from Seattle, Tacoma, Olympia, and Hoquiam. Each of the put up $500 for ownership of the company. Of the members, 63 were Swedish-speaking Finns and the rest were Swedes and Norwegians. But they all called themselves Americans.

Leadership was selected by the part-owners, each of whom had one vote. Everyone worked for four dollars a day, regardless of the job—a system not understood nor appreciated by the financial community. During the first eight months, no salaries were paid at all.

The first factory of the Olympia Veneer Company was a "fire sale" bargain, a burned-out sawmill near Tacoma that the owners bought for $7,000. They pitched in and rebuilt it, bought machinery on credit, and were ready for business by fall of their first year.

Almost none of the owners had any experience in veneer work. When their machines arrived, they had to hire outside help from Portland to demonstrate how to run them. Their first order—for cheap orange-packing crates—came from California. Everyone worked frantically for the first three months. But because some of that year's orange crop was ruined by a frost, cancellations came in, and the co-op wound up $19,000 short.

Capital was badly needed, so some of the owners tried without success to borrow from the banks. The Swedes had already taken what advances they could out of the company, but the Swedo-Finns left their money in—an action that saved the company. Many wives of the owners went to work elsewhere to earn money for the company. Finally it was decided that everybody would have to put up another $500 to buy stock, lumber, and other materials. But many had already put in their life savings; from then on they would have to borrow from friends and relatives and go without salaries.

At last orders began coming in, and the company showed small gains. Some of the loans were paid off, and in 1923 the company paid its first dividend—$300 per share. The following year, Olympia Veneer Company had total assets of $75,000, and the banker who had earlier turned down the loan request now offered to help in return for 50 percent of the stock. Needless to say, the offer was rejected. In 1954, after considering many offers to buy their holdings, the owners of Olympia Veneer decided to sell to the U.S. Plywood Company. Their total holdings, exchanged for stock in U.S. Plywood, were valued at $20 million.

The history of Olympia Veneer is a true success story—a story of the coming of age of an industry started by poor immigrants who, with hard work and sacrifice, built a thriving business in a new land. It is also a testimony to the energy and the dedication of the Swedo-Finns.

PART VII

Americanization

After Finland declared its independence from Russia in 1917, Finnish immigration to America never again reached the volume of previous periods. For the next few years, a number of Finns sailed to Canada, and some of the newer Finnish arrivals in America returned home. But those who had been in the United States long enough to put down roots stayed on and involved themselves in American life.

1. *The Melting Pot*

For a while the Finns in America held fast to their societies, newspapers, causes, traditions, and language. But gradually, much to the dismay of the older immigrants, things began to change. Their children started using American slang words, chewing gum, and wondering why they had to drink milk instead of soda pop. They began to request store-bought bread in their school lunch pails instead of mothers' home-baked rye. And they wanted American clothes instead of old-fashioned homemade things. Young men no longer wore their *pieksu* boots with the turned-up toes, and young women discarded their unfashionable shawls and homespun dresses for clothes from mail-order catalogs or drygoods stores. For a while, even the Finnish language seemed endangered, particularly during the 1920s and 1930s, when "melting pot" attitudes were so strong.

Today people have become aware of the importance of preserving unique ethnic customs and cultures. But in those days, people all over the country were taking up the idea that America was a "melting pot" in which all racial and ethnic groups were to shed their ancient heritages and become as one people — Americans. The Finns were not the only victims of this movement. It affected all groups, particularly minorities whose ways and languages were strikingly different from the majority of Americans. Some children were ashamed of their parents' heavy accents and old-fashioned ways. Many changed their names for simplicity's sake, or to avoid possible ridicule from those who had names easy to pronounce and spell.

Among the older immigrants, "melting" into American society was a slow process. Language remained a barrier, even though Old Country Finns struggled hard to learn English — or at least that's what they claimed. Some declared they were mastering one new English word each year, but most of them settled for a curious mixture of English and Finnish that the writer H. L. Mencken called "Finglish" in his book *The American Language*. It was an easy dialect for the immigrants to understand, and even non-Finns advertised their products in Finglish when they were selling in Finnish communities. As time went on, however, the dialect became so specialized that neither Americans nor Old Country Finns could understand it.

The Old Country Finns also had to struggle with another problem — that of homesickness for Finland. It was not so acute during the years when their children were growing up and everyone was working hard. Then, there wasn't so much time to miss the birch forests, the fragrant spring flowers, or the cuckoos singing in the woodlands. Most families had learned to appreciate the climate in America and had adjusted to life in a country that had no midnight sun in June. But as people grew older, nostalgia gnawed at them; they longed to return to Finland.

Older Finnish immigrants like this farm woman from Michigan were often homesick for the life they had left behind in Finland.

Some of their unhappiness stemmed from guilt about having left in the first place. Then, too, they knew they faced disapproval from the people back home. In the early days, this was expressed in sayings such as "Never trust a Finn who is living abroad" or "Once one has crossed the ocean once, he is always on the wrong side." Nevertheless, they did go home, often seven or eight times, before America finally "took." These travelers became known as "birds of passage." With today's jet travel, there is a constant stream of such "birds" among second- and third-generation Finns who love to see places they've always heard about as youngsters.

But the longer the new settlers were away, the more evident it became that they belonged on the western side of the ocean. They were content to be Americans.

For many Finns, being American meant getting involved in politics. Finnish-American women, in particular, were enthusiastic boosters for the right to vote. In 1906, Finland had become the first country in Europe (and the second in the world after

New Zealand) to grant women that right. Finnish-American women participated enthusiastically in colorful parades for the cause of woman suffrage in New York, Minneapolis, Duluth, and other cities. The suffragists also founded their own newspaper, *Toveritar*, in Astoria, Oregon, in 1907 — a daring move for that day and age.

Early Finnish-Americans were almost solidly Republican. They somehow associated the Democratic party with hard times. Said one old timer, "I have always voted for the Republicans and I always will, so long as my eyes see the blue of the heavens and my ears hear the echoes of the backwoods." The Republican president William McKinley was a great favorite of the immigrants. Once, they lovingly sent him a pair of slippers and a $500 gold and silver memento. Teddy Roosevelt, another hero, received a beautiful hand-made *puukko* sheathed knife.

But times changed, and by 1932 most Finns, both conservative and liberal, were supporting Democrat Franklin Delano Roosevelt. Today, Finnish-Americans seem to follow no particular voting pattern.

2. *Crosscurrents*

During the great emigrations from Finland, many Finns who stayed behind were critical of life in America. But Finnish emigrants who returned to Finland as visitors from America soon changed attitudes in the Old Country. It was obvious that they had made something of their lives and had found opportunities across the sea that simply hadn't existed in Finland. The two groups of Finns — those who had stayed, and those who had left — became better friends. American Finns took great pride in sending gifts back to Finland — Chinook salmon spawn from Astoria, Oregon, white-tailed deer from Minnesota, grouse from Wisconsin, and many seeds and plants. Now, there are even red deer from Virginia thriving in Finnish forests.

In addition, the United States and Finland were fast friends at the government level. America had loaned money to Finland and to other European countries during World War I, and Finland was the only country to conscientiously pay back her loan. In 1949, President Harry S. Truman arranged for the repaid loan to be converted into a scholarship fund that would enable 80 Finnish students to study in the United States each year. In 1952, these scholarships were incorporated into the expanded Fulbright-Hays Exchange Program. Betwen the years 1949 and 1971, 467 Americans studied in Finland, while 1,487 Finns were educated in the United States. By June 1971, 40 former Fulbright scholars had become college teachers in Finland.

Trade between the two countries flourished during the 1920s. Finland imported American automobiles, machinery, hardware, metals, and raw cotton, while the United States imported Finnish cellulose, paper, and woodworking products. Trade dwindled after the Great Depression but picked up again in 1936, when Finland became one of 16 nations to sign a mutually profitable trade agreement with the United States. Today, in addition to trading with Finland, some 70 American companies have established trade relations with the Soviet Union using Finnish companies as agents, distributors, and service centers.

During the early years of Finnish-American relations, many cultural and social ties bound the two countries. The music of Finnish composer Jean Sibelius thrilled American audiences, and Paavo Nurmi, the "Flying Finn," became a household word as he broke Olympic track records. In Finland, American novels and plays attracted a wide audience. Eugene O'Neill's plays, for example, were translated into Finnish and performed in Helsinki theaters.

Friendship between the Finns and the Americans flourished for many years as cultural, social, and economic ties became stronger. But with the coming of World War II, an event occurred

that really brought out the Finnish-Americans' love for the
mother country. This was Soviet Russia's attack on Finland in
1939 — the Winter War.

Although the United States was officially neutral, there was no
doubt as to the American people's sympathies. Former President
Herbert Hoover spoke out strongly on behalf of the Finns, whom
he had long admired. When Congress failed to act on his recom-
mendations to break diplomatic relations with the Soviets, he
established a fund-raising organization for the relief of the Finns
made homeless by the war. In New York City, Mayor Fiorello
LaGuardia formed a committee to sponsor a "Let's Help Finland"
mass meeting in Madison Square Garden on December 20, 1939.

Other groups rushed to offer aid. The American Red Cross
appropriated $25,000 for initial relief measures; an additional

Finnish-Americans pack medicine and clothing
to be sent to Finland during the Winter War.

$10,000 was immediately sent to London for the purchase of medicines to be flown to the Finnish Red Cross. All Red Cross chapters in the United States were urged to collect contributions for the relief of Finnish war victims. Meanwhile, American-Finnish clubs and associations formed a relief committee, composed of 39 societies, and set a goal of $1 million to be raised for the Finnish Red Cross.

At the Finnish Workers Educational Alliance, huge cartons packed with old clothes and shoes and labeled with the Red Cross emblem were shipped to war sufferers. From various parts of the United States, men of Finnish origin, eager to aid in Finland's defense, headed for New York and the ships that would take them abroad. There were women volunteers, too—nurses and others eager to do war work—who went to Finland on the Swedish liner *Gripsholm*. Four Finnish seamen jumped ship at Portland, Maine, and made their way to New York, where they could sail on the *Gripsholm* with the other volunteers. An American pilot signed on, hoping he could organize a Finnish-American flying corps.

Probably at no time in American history had the public been so concerned about the fate of a small foreign country. But not enough help came in time, and Finland was forced to give part of its territory to Russia after 105 days of bitter fighting.

Finland's close ties with the United States, however, continued to flourish after the war. New immigrants flew across the ocean in a matter of hours instead of sailing for days and days. Many wore fine clothes rather than homespun costumes, and carried smart luggage in place of knapsacks and crudely tied boxes. The majority spoke several languages, although English was sometimes their poorest, and a sizeable percentage were accomplished artists, scholars, technicians, businessmen, and professional people.

A number of Finns who were already established in America resettled during and after World War II. Thousands left their

The Finnish-American Rest Home in Lake Worth, Florida, provides a home for retired people of Finnish ancestry.

"Finntowns" and family farms in the north to serve in the military or in defense jobs in distant cities. During the 1940s and 1950s, many developed a great fondness for Florida sunshine, particularly when it came time for retirement. Lake Worth-Lantana, in Palm Beach County, now has a permanent Finnish population of about 15,000, which nearly doubles during the winter months. There are two weekly radio programs in Finnish, two large halls, and three churches, all supported by the Finnish community. Since the 1960s, immigrants have been arriving in Florida directly from Finland.

By the 1970s, the exchange of people, ideas, and culture between Finland and America had been underway for more than 300 years. When the American Bicentennial Administration began planning the country's big 1976 "birthday" celebration,

Finnish-Americans responded enthusiastically with the formation of their own U.S.A. bicentennial group. Almost simultaneously, the Republic of Finland became one of the first nations to offer substantial participation in the bicentennial. The goal was to establish educational, cultural, and artistic exchanges that would make the Finnish-American contribution to American life better known to all Americans. With a "cast of thousands"—workers, performers, artists, planners, fund-raisers, and patriotic boosters—the Finnish-American community dedicated itself to the bicentennial spirit.

Today Finland's gifts to the United States are more widely appreciated than ever before. People from all walks of life are familiar with things made in Finland. Cross-country ski enthusiasts step onto Finnish-made skis as they set out across the snow, while outdoorsmen make use of several models of *puukko* knives. Fishermen attach Finnish-made lures to their lines, and seamstresses cut patterns out of Finnish-designed fabrics with scissors made in Finland. Finnish design concepts, which follow the idea that "simple, plus practical, equals beautiful," are evident in the handsome furniture and glassware that have become so popular in the United States.

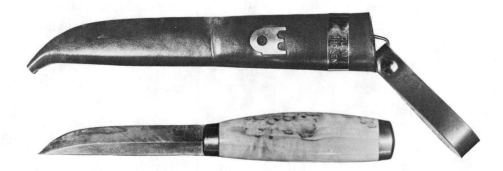

The versatile *puukko* knife, shown here with a leather sheath

Finnish products like these beautifully designed goblets and candlesticks from the Iittala Glassworks in Helsinki are very popular in the United States.

Many Finnish-Americans are now digging into their family histories to trace the stories of how their ancestors came to America and contributed to its growth. They take pride in their heritage. And they, along with other Americans of all backgrounds, have come to see that America is not a melting pot where various ethnic groups are mere ingredients in a "stew." Instead, it is a mosaic of strong, vital cultures—cultures, like that of Finland, that have much to contribute to the American way of life.

"Old Main," a building at Suomi College in Hancock, Michigan.
About a third of the students at Suomi are of Finnish origin.

PART VIII

Contributions to American Life

Finnish-Americans are active in every area of American life. Many have become outstanding in their chosen fields.

1. *Education*

Many Finnish immigrant families placed great importance on educating their children in America. Perhaps as a result, many of these children went on to pursue outstanding careers in the field of education. One such person is Dr. Ralph J. Jalkanen, president of Suomi College in Hancock, Michigan. Dr. Jalkanen's parents emigrated from Finland in 1910. They settled in Coburntown, a community in Upper Michigan, where Ralph's father worked a 10-hour day at the Quincy mine. The family kept cows, and young Ralph helped sell milk to supplement the family income. His mother took in boarders. After his father died, Ralph, then 16, worked hard during summer vacations to help keep the family going.

Ralph was always a serious student at school. He pursued musical studies and became an accomplished pianist, but he was always most interested in religion and higher education. After graduating from Suomi College, he went on to Elmhurst College, where he received his bachelor of arts degree. He received a bachelor of divinity degree from Suomi Theological Seminary in 1943, and a master of arts degree in psychology from Roosevelt College of Arts and Sciences in Chicago. Dr. Jalkanen continued his graduate studies at the University of Chicago and Loyola University, Chicago, where he received a doctorate in philosophy.

As an author and editor, Dr. Jalkanen has written numerous articles and reports as well as two important books, *The Finns in North America: A Social Symposium* and *The Faith of the Finns: Historical Perspectives on the Finnish Lutheran Church in America*. He recently contributed to a volume entitled *Finland Salutes the U.S.A. — Old Friends — Strong Ties*, which was published in Finland in honor of the American bicentennial.

In tribute to Dr. Jalkanen's leadership among Americans of Finnish descent, the Republic of Finland, in 1971, bestowed upon him its highest award, the Order of the Lion Commanders Medal.

Another educator whose parents emigrated from Finland is Dr. Jacob W. Heikkinen, professor of the New Testament at Lutheran Theological Seminary in Gettysburg, Pennsylvania, and director of the Lutheran House of Studies in Washington, D.C. He is the youngest of seven sons born to Herman and Amanda Heikkinen. "My father was a tailor by trade," says Dr. Heikkinen. "He came from Finland to Upper Michigan for adventure... but my mother emigrated from Suomussalmi out of sheer necessity. Her family was large, and from the age of 12 she had to make her own way in the world. She worked in America for two years to pay for her passage...."

The Heikkinen family moved to Michigan in 1899. Life was hard, but the Heikkinens were equal to the challenge. Even with

Dr. Ralph J. Jalkanen   **Dr. Jacob W. Heikkinen**

all the privations and difficulties, Herman lived to be 82, and Amanda never required medical attention until the end of her life at age 92.

Dr. Heikkinen inherited his parents' spirit and energy. Following World War II, he traveled to Finland to serve as administrator of a million-dollar reconstruction program sponsored by the American Lutheran Church. He has also served as president of the Washington, D.C., chapter of the Finlandia Foundation.

Dr. Heikkinen's wife, Toini, is one of four sisters whose parents emigrated from Ostrobothnia in Finland. Her father was a mill worker in western Pennsylvania. An accomplished pianist, church organist, and music teacher at Gettysburg College, Toini did her undergraduate work at Oberlin College and received her master's degree from Peabody Institute in Baltimore, Maryland.

Professor John I. Kolehmainen, another educator born of Finnish immigrant parents, was a member of the faculty of Heidelberg College in Ohio from 1937 until his recent retirement. As chairman of the Department of Politics and Government, he contributed greatly to the education of young people, both as lecturer and as historian.

Dr. Kolehmainen is generally recognized as the dean of Finnish-American immigrant studies. His book *Epic of the North*, the story of Finland's national folk epic, *The Kalevala*, won second prize in the 1972 Chicago Folklore competition. A bibliography of his extensive writings on Finland and the American Finns was published in 1971 by the Aigler Fund of Heidelberg College. For his outstanding contributions, he was honored by the Finnish government with the Order of the Finnish Lion First Class and the Medal of the Golden Jubilee Independence of Finland.

Professor Jorma Kalliokoski, one of America's outstanding geologists, was born in Finland and emigrated with his family to Ontario, Canada, in 1930. His father, a carpenter, enjoyed reading history and wrote poetry in later life. His mother had a number of stories published by the leading Finnish-Canadian newspaper *Vapaa Sana*. Jorma was educated in the United States, and in 1951, received his Ph.D. from Princeton University. In 1952, he moved permanently to the United States, becoming a citizen in 1968.

Dr. Kalliokoski was on the Princeton faculty from 1956 through 1968. During those years, he spent five summers studying the geology and the mineral resources of the north-central Guayana Shelf of Venezuela. Dr. Kalliokoski was also one of the organizers of the 1963 Princeton University Conference entitled "The Role of National Governments in the Exploration of Mineral Resources." In 1968, he was appointed chairman of the Department of Geology and Geological Engineering at Michigan Technological University in Houghton. He is also business editor for the magazine *Economic Geology.*

Dr. Allan Kuusisto, another distinguished Finnish-American

Dr. John I. Kolehmainen   **Dr. Jorma Kalliokoski**   **Dr. Allan Kuusisto**

educator, is president of the Hobart and William Smith Colleges in Geneva, New York. Before taking this position, he served as vice president for academic affairs of the State University of New York at Albany. He was also a professor of government at the University of New Hampshire between 1948 and 1961.

2. *Public Service*

Finnish-Americans have always been actively involved in community affairs. On the business letterhead of one Finnish-American, Kalevi Olkio, is this simple message: "Every man should give something of himself to his community—and to his fellow man." And the people of Baltimore, Maryland, as well as sailors visiting that eastern port, can testify to the fact that this jovial, energetic man practices exactly what he preaches.

Kalevi, who left Finland when he was 16 years old, was a sailor for about 11 years aboard Finnish, Norwegian, and Swedish ships. During World War II he was a deck officer on

American transports. In 1946, he was forced to stay in Baltimore for two months while his ship was undergoing repairs. He didn't like the waterfront much, but he "...found the city itself fascinating. The people were very nice, very friendly...." He sailed for home, but got only as far as Stockholm before the irresistible urge to return to America took over. He went back and settled in Baltimore.

Kalevi, who speaks Finnish, English, Norwegian, Danish, Swedish, Spanish, and German, is many things to many people. Basically he earns a living by selling electrical equipment to ships. But he also supplies hospitality and friendship at no cost at all. One Norwegian captain said of him, "Olkio is the best Norwegian in Baltimore...even if he is a Finn!" Olkio understands seamen and their problems; he makes sure that they find the YMCA if they want a swim, or he tells them where to find a good meal and a clean bed. What Kalevi Olkio does, in fact, is to sell America and, in particular, Baltimore.

Kalevi publishes booklets and brochures in Norwegian and English for his friends, the seamen. Most of them contain advice, information, and notes of welcome to the visitors. He is very active in ethnic groups around Baltimore. He has been president of the Sons of Norway and editor of the Nordkap *News*. Currently he is president of the Baltimore chapter of the Finlandia Foundation. He envisions the Baltimore waterfront as becoming an ethnic showcase, with each national group—Polish Ukrainian, Filipino, Norwegian, Estonian, and others—opening shops, restaurants, and specialty businesses identified in the native languages as well as in English.

Another Finnish-American who has contributed greatly to her community is Irene Waisanen, a Michigan newspaper editor. Irene was born in a Finnish community in Michigan. She received excellent tutoring from her mentor, Professor Waino Lehto, during her college days at Suomi College in Hancock. In 1944, she began working for the *Daily Mining Gazette* in Houghton, Michigan, and she became the newspaper's editor in 1964. In addition to her editorial work, Irene is very active in community affairs. She has received recognition for promoting a number of community projects, including the Upper Peninsula Michigan State Fair. She was the first woman director of the Copper Country Chamber of Commerce, a position she held for three years. An honorary member of the Copper Kiwanis Club, she promotes tourism and holiday festivals in the Copper Country, community projects for people of all ages, health programs, and any projects she feels are beneficial to the community. She is also an active supporter of Suomi College and Michigan Technological University.

Another Finnish-American woman, Dr. Anna Elonen, has spent a lifetime serving the public through her work in medicine.

Kalevi Olkio

Dr. Anna Elonen

Dr. Elonen came to America from Finland when she was nine years old. She studied at the universities of Minnesota and Chicago, graduating with a doctorate in clinical psychology. Dr. Elonen served as a clinician in the department of psychiatry at the University of Michigan for many years, until her recent retirement. She has done extensive work in America and in Finland in the area of psychological diagnosis and treatment of handicapped children.

3. *Military Service*

One Finnish-American who has distinguished himself in the armed services is Lieutenant Commander Marlin Wiita, right wingman of the famed Navy precision flying team known as the Blue Angels. Marlin was born of Finnish-American parents in Aitken, Minnesota. When he was nine, his family moved to Fairbanks, Alaska, which he now considers his permanent home.

Lieutenant Commander Marlin Wiita

Rear Admiral Onnie P. Lattu

LCDR Wiita holds 17 Air Medals, 4 Navy Commendation Medals with Combat "V," 2 Meritorious Unit Commendations, the Vietnamese Cross of Gallantry, and the Vietnam Service and Campaign Medals.

Rear Admiral Onnie P. Lattu, USN (Ret.), was born in Hitola, Finland. His parents brought him to Fort Bragg, California, when he was a youngster. Admiral Lattu has had a long and distinguished naval career that has taken him to Europe and the Pacific. The much decorated admiral continues to be active in Finnish-American cultural activities.

4. *Entertainment*

One Finnish-American who has made great contributions in the field of entertainment is Taina Elg, a Finnish-born actress and ballet dancer whose career began with the National Opera Company in Helsinki, Finland. She was awarded a scholarship to the famed Royal Ballet School in London, after which she joined the Marquis de Cuevas Company in Paris and Monte Carlo. A minor accident caused her to leave the ballet company temporarily, and she filled in the time as a high-fashion model in Paris. Finally, she was signed on at MGM in Hollywood for featured roles in several films. She was then given starring roles in such movies as *Les Girls, Watusi, Imitation General*, and *The 39 Steps.*

Ms. Elg has also served as a guest artist in many American television series. On stage, she has appeared in productions such as *Redhead, Silk Stockings, Can Can, West Side Story*, and *Look to the Lilies.* In 1972-73, Taina Elg co-starred in the national touring company production of *Two By Two*, and in 1974, she performed in Australia, where, for almost a year, she appeared in *A Little Night Music.* In 1975, Ms. Elg was nominated for a Tony Award for her performance in *Where's Charley*, and was seen on television's highly acclaimed "Adams Chronicles."

Taina Elg

Albert Salmi

Albert Salmi, an actor familiar to many for his role in the television series "Petrocelli," has done well in American theater. The son of Finnish parents, he began his career on Broadway, starring in the hit play *Bus Stop*. His first role in motion pictures was that of Smerdyakov in the movie version of Dostoevsky's novel *The Brothers Karamazov*. Since that time, Salmi has been featured in many other films and has made more than 100 guest appearances in television dramas.

5. *Music*

A number of Finnish-Americans have made a lasting mark in the world of music in the United States. Martti Nisonen, from Pori, Finland, taught music for many years at Suomi College. Before coming to America he had gained popularity as a conductor of light opera in Helsinki. At Suomi College he composed a symphony based on an American Indian theme, an oratorio, several cantatas, and a choral arrangement for the whole of Finnish composer Jean Sibelius' *Finlandia*. The great composer approved of the arrangement wholeheartedly, and the Detroit Symphony has performed it before enthusiastic audiences.

Charles Wuorinen, whose father emigrated from Finland in 1916, is an outstanding modern composer, conductor, and pianist. He has received numerous awards, honors, and commissions, including a Pulitzer Prize, two Guggenheim fellowships, and a National Institute of Arts and Letters Award. Along with Harvey Sollberger, he is the co-founder and co-director of the Group for Contemporary Music. Mr. Wuorinen is on the faculty at Columbia University in New York, where he composes and performs.

Charles Wuorinen

95

Kaija Juusela, a singer who received her musical education at the Sibelius Academy of Helsinki, came to the United States in 1957 and studied under the famous baritone Todd Duncan. She first sang with the Opera Society of Washington in 1959. Since then she has appeared in various productions of the Opera Society, singing solo parts in *L'Enfant et les Sortileges, Madame Butterfly, Werther, Mahagony,* and *The Magic Flute.* She works as a permanent soloist for a number of Washington, D.C., area churches, and appears as a soloist in numerous concerts.

6. *The Arts*

Many Finnish-Americans have excelled in painting and wood carving, and especially in sculpture. One world-renowned painter, Johan William (Juho) Rissanen, was born in Finland but in 1938 moved to Florida, where he spent the last 12 years of his life. Exhibitions of his paintings have been held in almost all the European capitals, as well as in Asia. In America, the Finnish-American Historical Society commissioned Juho Rissanen to paint a fresco depicting the life of a Finnish immigrant family on a Minnesota farm. Reproductions of this much-beloved work hang in thousands of Finnish-American homes.

Kauko Rissanen, a nephew of Juho, is an artist of a different sort. He specializes in portraits carved in wood. Trained in oil painting, interior decorating, sculpting, and wood carving at the Helsinki Athenaeum Art School, he completed his first portrait, that of Marshal Mannerheim, while in the service during World War II. His next subject was King Gustav V of Sweden. In 1956 Rissanen moved to the United States, and now he and his wife are American citizens. He has been commissioned to do portraits of President Kekkonen of Finland, as well as of several American presidents and many other prominent Americans.

The sculptor Kalervo Kallio, son of Finland's fourth president, came to the United States in 1949. In Finland, he had become

Kauko Rissanen works on one of his portraits in wood.

famous for his portrait busts of several composers, including Jean Sibelius, as well as for his various statues and war memorials. He had also sculpted busts of three Finnish presidents and two of Finland's Nobel Prize winners. Kallio gained initial fame in America when his portrait of America's first secretary of defense, James Forrestal, won an international competition in Washington, D.C. The bust is now displayed in the Mall entrance to the Pentagon.

Kallio was highly accomplished in sculpting portraits out of marble, granite, diorite, and nickel-ore. Among his subjects were presidents Harry S. Truman and Herbert Hoover, and scientist Albert Einstein. Kallio's bust of Vice President Alben Barkley is housed in the gallery of the vice presidents in the Capitol Building in Washington, D.C. His bust of General George C.

Marshall was unveiled at the Marshall Space Flight Center in Huntsville, Alabama, by President Eisenhower and Mrs. George Marshall. In 1960, Kallio went to Africa to do a bust of Dr. Albert Schweitzer.

Kalvero Kallio (second from left) presents a model of his bust of James Forrestal to government and army officials.

One of the most beautiful works of Finnish sculpture in America is Wäinö Aaltonen's granite memorial to the Finns who first colonized the Delaware River area. This memorial was made possible by the efforts of another dedicated Finnish-American, Dr. John M. Leekala. Dr. Leekala, whose parents emigrated from Finland, has devoted most of his life to studying the details of the Finns' historical role in colonial America.

Wäinö Aaltonen's memorial to the early Finnish settlers in Delaware

In addition to contributing to the visual arts, Finns have also done some work in the literary field. Jingo Viitala Vachon, a writer, is well known for her humorous reminiscences of her childhood in the Upper Peninsula of Michigan. Her first book, *Tall Timber Tales*, was published in 1973. These delightful stories of life in the big timber area of the Upper Peninsula were followed by *Sagas from Sisula*, which tells of her early childhood in a large Finnish family of 40 or 50 years ago.

Jingo Viitala Vachon

Although her books and humorous newspaper columns have made her known in many states of the union, Jingo and her husband choose to live quietly in a relatively unsettled area near Toivola, Michigan, the scene of many of her stories.

7. *Architecture*

Although the Finnish log cabin will always remain a unique part of early America's colonial architecture, the works of contemporary Finnish architects stand in a class by themselves as timeless masterpieces of design.

Alvar Aalto, friend of the famous American architect Frank Lloyd Wright, was one of the greatest of the Finnish architects. He was essentially a national architect whose major works stand in Finland and in other European countries. The model city that he helped design in Tapiola, Finland, has attracted architects and city planners from all over the world. Americans first saw his work in the Finnish Pavillion at the New York World's Fair in 1939. His imaginative use of timber construction with free-flowing lines earned him a professorship at the Massachusetts Institute of Technology in 1940. Shortly after World War II, Aalto designed Baker House, a senior dormitory at M.I.T., in a bold new style that was quite different from old colonial forms. In 1964, he designed the Kaufman Conference Room in New York, and in 1970, the library at Mount Angel Benedictine Abbey in Oregon. In keeping with his philosophy that an architect must

The interior of the library at Mount Angel Abbey, designed by **Alvar Aalto**

understand and coordinate even the smallest accessories of an environment, Aalto is also famed for his furniture designs, marketed under the name *Artek*.

Eliel Saarinen, another great architect of Finnish birth, emigrated to Bloomfield Hills, Michigan, the year after he won second prize in the *Chicago Tribune* tower design competition in 1922. At Bloomfield Hills, he inspired and directed the Cranbrook Foundation's Academy of Art for 20 years. In addition to designing buildings at Cranbrook, he designed the performance halls at the Berkshire Music Center in Lenox, Massachusetts, and at Suomi College. He also collaborated with his son Eero in designing many buildings, including the Smithsonian Art Gallery in Washington, D.C., campus buildings at Antioch College in Ohio and Brandeis University in Massachusetts, and churches in Indiana and Minnesota.

Eliel Saarinen's wife, Louise, who had studied design in Helsinki and Paris, introduced Finnish weaving and fabric design to America by opening a department at Cranbrook Academy in 1927. With support from leading Finnish designers and artists from other countries, she set the stage for the famed exhibition "Cranbrook Weavers; Pacesetters and Prototypes," held at the Detroit Institute of Art in 1973.

The Saarinens' son, Eero, was born in 1910 at Kirkkonummi, Finland, and became a naturalized American citizen at the age of 13. After studying at Grande Chaumiere, Paris, and receiving his Bachelor of Fine Arts degree from Yale University, he worked with his father Eliel until the latter's death in 1950. His honors include Master of Arts, Yale University; Doctor of Humane Letters, Valparaiso University; Doctor of Humanities, Wayne University; Doctor of Engineering, Technische Hochschule, Hanover, Germany; Fellow, American Institute of Architects; Fellow, American Academy of Arts and Letters; and an A.I.A. Gold Medal Award in 1962.

Eero Saarinen

The younger Saarinen was interested in everything from lamps and other furniture to massive buildings and great arches. He participated in Organic Design Furniture, a Museum of Modern Art competition in 1938. For Knoll Associates, he designed the Plywood Chair in 1964, the Womb Chair in 1948, and Pedestal Furniture in 1958. He also designed furniture for the General Motors Technical Center lobbies in 1950.

But Saarinen's real genius is seen in his independent architectural designs, some of which were not actually built until after his death in 1961. Among his great architectural achievements were the Dulles Airport in Washington, D.C., the Deere & Company headquarters in Illinois, and the CBS tower in New York. The Jefferson National Expansion Memorial in St. Louis,

The Jefferson National Expansion Memorial

Missouri, "Gateway to the West," was also designed by Eero Saarinen. When one of his last buildings, the Beaumont Theater in New York City, was finished after his death, Wolf Von Eckardt wrote in the *Washington Post*, "It is only now, as his last designs are one by one turning into buildings, that the full measure of our loss is beginning to reveal itself."

Saarinen himself had a dramatic and inspiring view of architecture. "Great architecture," he once said, "is both universal and individual. The universality is achieved because the architecture is a true expression of its time. The individuality comes through as a result of a special quality.... This quality is the philosophy and thinking behind architecture. It is the expression of one man's unique combination of faith and honesty and devotion and beliefs in architecture, in short, his moral integrity."

The Finnish-American contribution to architecture has indeed been great. In addition to Aalto and the Saarinens, there have been many other fine architects, such as Elino Jyring, Reino Aarnio, K. Werner Haapala, Arnold Aho, and J. William Ilmanen.

8. *A Success Story*

Probably the most widely known member of the Finnish-American community is Dr. Vaino Hoover, whose success story best illustrates how children of poor immigrants could, and did, rise to prominence in America.

The saga begins in Finland, where Ernie Huovinen, a woodsman, and his wife, Maria Matilda Kosunen Huovinen, worked at various lumber camps. Ernie worked with an axe and saw, and Maria cooked and baked for the camp crews. In 1903, they decided that Ernie should go to America. There, he would work and save enough money to send for Maria and their five children. Maria helped to finance the venture by saving money she made as a camp cook and a weaver. The following year, the family sailed to America.

The Huovinens settled in Stray Horse Gulch near Leadville, Colorado. Maria ran a boarding house for Finnish miners, while Ernie worked as a timberman in the mines. He once left home for two years to work as a fruit picker in Cuba. After returning to Colorado, Ernie died in 1912, the victim of years of hard work.

Maria Huovinen moved to Wisconsin with her six children,

the youngest of whom was Vaino. The children grew up on a Wisconsin farm, and the older ones finally went their individual ways, leaving young Vaino and his mother at home. Vaino worked hard in sawmills and lumber camps, even when he was only of grammar school age. With the help of his high school principal, the young Finn took a home study course, which enabled him to continue working in the woods for badly needed income.

Between 1919 and 1923, he attended high school in Chicago and Hollywood, studying college preparatory courses in engineering while supporting himself by working evenings, weekends, and vacations as a telegraph messenger.

An outstanding student in physics, he was awarded a scholarship in electrical engineering at the California Institute of Technology. During that period, Vaino (who by then had Americanized his last name from Huovinen to Hoover) showed his athletic prowess by becoming the best javelin thrower the school had yet produced. He graduated with a bachelor of science degree in 1927, and in 1931 received his Ph.D. (Magna Cum Laude) in electrical engineering, physics, and mathematics.

Since that time, Dr. Hoover has been involved in the design and manufacture of electrical motor and generating machinery, control systems, and specialized equipment for mining, petroleum, chemical, and aircraft industries. For the past 35 years, the aircraft industry has benefited greatly from Dr. Hoover's designs. For the Lockheed C5A, he designed and manufactured high-powered, multiple-speed electric winches for handling heavy cargo containers and vehicles. Recently he has been involved in the design and manufacture of electric motor propulsion units and exploration equipment for deep submergence underwater vehicles.

Dr. Vaino Hoover from Stray Horse Gulch is as Finnish as they come. A sports enthusiast, he served as the National Chairman for the Finnish-American Olympic Fund Drive during the 1960,

Dr. Vaino Hoover

1964, 1968, and 1972 Olympic Games. He also served as the attaché for the Finnish Olympic Team during the 1960 Winter Olympic Games at Squaw Valley, California.

His pet projects involve helping Suomi College as a fund raiser and generous contributor, and promoting cultural and educational exchanges between Finland and America. He is national president of the Finlandia Foundation and national vice president of the American-Scandinavian Foundation. In short, he is a man who loves being an American, but who is proud of his Finnish heritage as well.

Finns like Dr. Hoover have contributed admirably to their adopted land, America. Today, Finnish-Americans are making a mark in almost every field and profession in the United States. Through their efforts from early colonial times to the present day, these energetic, creative people have made a lasting contribution to the strength and diversity of American society.

. . . INDEX . . .

ACKNOWLEDGMENTS

The illustrations are reproduced through the courtesy of: pp. 6, 10, 12, 13, 19, 23, 34, 38, 48, 54, 71, 82, National Museum of Finland, Helsinki; p. 16, United States Postal Service; p. 17, State of Delaware, Department of State, Division of Historical and Cultural Affairs, Dover, Delaware; p. 21, Pennsylvania Historical and Museum Commission, Pennsylvania State Archives; p. 27, State of Alaska, Department of Education; p. 29 (left and right), R.A. Pierce of Queen's University, Kingston, Canada; p. 30, Helsinki City Museum; pp. 37, 42, 52, 59, 68, Historical Museum of Turku, Institute for Migration, University of Turku, Finland; pp. 45, 51, Michigan Technological University Library Archives; p. 46, International Museum of Photography at George Eastman House; pp. 50, 65, Immigration History Research Center, University of Minnesota; p. 56, Minnesota Historical Society Archives; pp. 61, 62, Jack Heino, Midland Cooperatives Incorporated, Superior, Wisconsin; pp. 66, 84, 87 (left), 107, Suomi College Archives; p. 69, Minneapolis Tribune; p. 76, Peter Oikarinen; p. 79, United Press International; p. 81, Anne Jakola and Sunset Studio; p. 83, Consulate General of Finland, New York; p. 87 (right), Jacob W. Heikkinen; p. 89 (left), Heidelberg College; p. 89 (center), Jorma Kalliokoski; p. 89 (right), Hobart and William Smith Colleges; p. 91 (left), Kalevi Olkio; p. 91 (right), Anna Elonen; p. 92 (left and right), United States Navy; p. 94 (left), Taina Elg; p. 94 (right), National Broadcasting Company, Incorporated; p. 95, Ruth Uebel Agency; p. 97, Lauri A. Paananen; p. 98, United States Army; p. 99, Delaware County Historical Society; p. 100, Jingo Viitala Vachon; p. 101, Morley Baer, Monterey, California; p. 103, Kevin Roche, John Dinkeloo and Associates, Hamden, Connecticut; p. 104, National Park Service.

ABOUT THE AUTHOR . . .

ELOISE ENGLE is a professional writer with a special interest in Finnish history and in the experiences of Finnish-Americans. Among her numerous published titles is an historical account of the famous Winter War between Finland and Russia, which was published by Charles Scribner's Sons in 1973. This book was co-authored by her husband, Lauri A. Paananen, who was born in Finland. Ms. Engle has also written many books for young people, one of which won an award as an outstanding science book for children in 1972. A member of such professional organizations as the American Society of Journalists and Authors and the Author's Guild, Ms. Engle is also active in the Finlandia Foundation and other Finnish-American cultural groups. She and her husband make their home in Falls Church, Virginia.

The IN AMERICA *Series*

We specialize in publishing quality books for
young people. For a complete list please write:

Lerner Publications Company
241 First Avenue North, Minneapolis, Minnesota 55401